OUR JEWISH FRIENDS

OUR JEWISH FRIENDS

BY
LOUIS GOLDBERG

MOODY PRESS
CHICAGO

All scripture quotations, except those noted otherwise, are
from the *New American Standard Bible,* © 1960,
1962, 1963, 1968, 1971, 1972, 1973, 1975 by The Lockman
Foundation, and are used by permission.

Library of Congress Cataloging in Publication Data

Goldberg, Louis, 1923-
   Our Jewish friends.

   1. Judaism.   2. Missions to Jews.   I. Title.

BM580.G58   253.7   76-56773

ISBN 0-8024-6217-0

Printed in the United States of America

CONTENTS

GUIDE FOR PRONUNCIATION OF
TRANSLITERATIONS

Hebrew transliterations given in this book represent modern Hebrew spoken in Israel today. The following are explanations of the symbols used in the transliteration of characters that have no corresponding letter in the English aphabet.

' —*aleph,* for all practical purposes, does not have a vocal sound.

ḥ —*ḥet* is a strongly whispered *h,* produced by tightening the throat muscles, as in the German *ach.*

ṭ —*ṭet* is pronounced as *t* in *Tom,* but another letter of the Hebrew alphabet, *tav,* also has the *t* sound.

' —*ain* is a voiced *ḥ,* produced when the vocal chords are set vibrating by the outgoing breath; however, in modern Hebrew the ' is not distinguished from '.

ṣ —*tzadi* is pronounced as a *ts,* as in *tsetse.*

PREFACE

THE NEED FOR UNDERSTANDING

The material in this book was originally taught to a number of churches, conference programs, and student groups. It is designed to introduce and acquaint Christians with the historical development, beliefs, customs, and practices of Judaism and the Jewish people. It includes material which explains how Christians can share basic biblical doctrines of the Hebrew Scriptures and the New Testament with their Jewish friends.

Christians need to better understand Jewish folk. The need is emphasized when we realize that almost one-half of the population of world Jewry lives in the United States. One of these Jewish people may very well be your neighbor. Understanding and accepting the Jewish person as your neighbor and friend will help you to share a New Testament faith in his Messiah with a sense of dignity as well as in an atmosphere of understanding.

Some Christians feel no need to learn how to communicate with Jewish people in terms of Jewish culture, history, and practice. Yet they can comprehend perfectly the need to learn to communicate similarly in such countries as Africa, South America, or the islands of the sea. Why do some Christians feel that we should preach the Gospel to Jewish people without realizing the Jewish culture of the gospels and using it? Christian faith sharing can be made more effective if presented from the Jewish context and with the recognition that our Jewish friends have their dignity as human beings and observe a religious practice that is based on their understanding of the Hebrew Scriptures.

This book is sent forth with the hope that there will be greater opportunity for sympathetic Jewish-Christian understanding and, through mutual concern, greater love for the Messiah of Israel. A bibliography of pertinent books, filmstrips, and films for further study is given at the close of each chapter. A catalog of source books for the Jewish festivals, Jewish culture, and Israel may be obtained from the American Association for Jewish Education, 114 Fifth Avenue, New York, N.Y. 10015.

This presentation is for the Christian's study of basic knowledge about the Jewish people. After this material has been grasped, a good course of study to use in faith sharing is Moody Correspondence School's *A Trumpet in Zion*. This Home Study Bible Course may be obtained by sending $3.00 plus 50¢ for postage and handling to Moody Correspondence School, 820 N. LaSalle St., Chicago, Illinois, 60610.

1

DEVELOPMENT AND DIVISIONS
OF JUDAISM

INTRODUCTION

In order to properly relate to our Jewish friends, it is quite important that we know something of the development and divisions of Judaism. A knowledge of some of the background of the Jewish people serves as a bridge of understanding to the Jewish heart and makes possible a better grasp of the Bible within the Jewish context.

On one occasion in the classroom, a passing reference was made to the Spanish-Jewish period. Someone in the back row thought that statement was the "cutest thing" he had ever heard; and he said, "Whoever heard of a Spanish Jew!" We had to stop at that point and explain to the class that this was a very important phase and factor in Jewish history. The Spanish period was one of the golden ages of Jewish literature. One little remark like that to a Jewish person, instead of building a bridge to a Jewish heart, would have raised a barrier. So we want to take a quick look at Judaism's development and divisions.

Obviously, the few brief pages at our disposal will not permit more than noting some of the main highlights of the story of Judaism. Today there are three main divisions and several subdivisions of Judaism, but at one time Juda-

ism was not so pluralistic. Judaism had its formative period
from 400 B.C.E. to 500 C.E.[1]

DEVELOPMENT OF ORTHODOXY: 400 B.C.E.—500 C.E.

The development of what we know today as the basic traditional practice of Judaism took place during the period
of 400 B.C.E. to 500 C.E.

EZRA AND THE SOPHERIM

One of the first men responsible for the training of a body
of scholars in the initial phase of the development period
was Ezra. This is the Ezra of the Bible, who came from
Babylon in 458 B.C.E., bringing a number of scholars with
him. They settled in the land of Israel and followed a number of scholarly pursuits. Ezra was responsible for the biblical books of Ezra, Chronicles, and probably Nehemiah.

But he was also responsible for the transliteration of the
Hebrew Scriptures,[2] that is, putting the Hebrew script of
the Scriptures into the Aramaic square characters and still
reading Hebrew. The reason for this was the change of
language: before the exile people used Hebrew, but after
the exile most of the common people spoke Aramaic. Ezra's
transliteration made it possible for people to pronounce in
Hebrew while using the Aramaic method of writing.

Ezra was also responsible for training a corps of teachers,
or scholars, called Sopherim, "bookmen," or "scribes."[3]
The Sopherim were the main religious leaders. In Ezra's

1. This is the Jewish designation of the year. The Jewish people do
   not refer to A.D., because it stands for *anno Domini* ("in the year of
   our Lord"). Jewish people do not say that Jesus is their Lord; therefore, they use the designation, C.E., "common era." Years prior to
   the common era are, then, B.C.E., "before the common era," instead
   of B.C., "before Christ."
2. *Hebrew Scriptures* is the term used by Jewish people in reference to
   the Old Testament. It is used throughout this book. The Christian
   should learn Jewish terminology to communicate better when speaking to Jewish people.
3. Sopherim were the religious leaders of this period. They are not to
   be confused with the scribes of the New Testament, who had the
   function of copying Scriptures.

day these men translated and explained the Scriptures, and we see them in action during Nehemiah's ministry (Neh 8:7-8), giving the sense of the Scriptures. These exegeses of the Word became, eventually, the *Targumim* tradition and were the start of Jewish tradition early in the intertestamental period. The explanations were carried as a body of oral material until they were written down about 180 c.e.

In the third century b.c.e. the Jewish authorities gave permission for a Greek translation of their Scriptures. This translation is known as the Septuagint.

THE MACCABEES AND THE HASIDIM

The next phase of development, 200-135 b.c.e., involves Maccabees and Hasidim. The story of the Maccabees represents a heroic phase in the history of the Jewish people. It is still remembered today in the holiday of Hanukkah.[4] The original family of Maccabees was responsible for the struggle for independence against the Syrians during 175-135 b.c.e. In the revolt, Israel eventually won her political independence as well as religious freedom.

The Hasidim ("pious ones," "devout ones") were the religious leaders in this period. They fought for religious freedom (won c. 164 b.c.e.) but, for the most part, abstained from fighting in the struggle for political freedom.

PHARISEES AND SADDUCEES

By the time we come to 135 b.c.e., we see two well-defined parties in Israel: Pharisees and Sadducees.

The Pharisees were the spiritual heirs of the original Sopherim, whom Ezra trained, as well as the later Hasidim. The Pharisees were noted for their separatist stand in an adherence to the development and practice of Judaism. We are too accustomed to thinking of only one brand of Pharisee, that represented in Luke 18:9-14 (the story of the

---

4. Hanukkah occurs around Christmas time (see chap. 3). Jesus observed this holiday when He was in Jerusalem (Jn 10:22-23).

Pharisee and the publican). But we must emphasize that not all Pharisees were like this one. There was a wide diversity of opinion among the Pharisees; some have said that there were as many as seven branches in the Pharisee party. These ranged all the way from the very legalistic (which the New Testament occasionally point out) to those who, like Gamaliel, were mystical, spiritually minded men (a branch the New Testament also indicates). Men such as Hillel (d. 10 B.C.E.) made up the latter group. We must recognize the wide variety there was among the Pharisees.

The Pharisees were responsible for the futher development of mainstream Judaism. Contemporary Orthodox Judaism is largely the product of the efforts of these men. The Pharisees were respected, or at least noted, by the people as *the* religious leaders.

The other group was the Sadducees, composed of the Maccabees and many priests. They were the rationalists of the day. These men denied the oral traditions, accepting only the written Word, especially the five books of Moses. They would have nothing to do with the traditions of mainstream Judaism, and on this point they clashed with the Pharisees. One example of this sharp divergence was the occasion when Paul defended himself before the council. When he realized his precarious position, he shouted his belief in the resurrection, after noting the presence of both Pharisees and Sadducees on the council (Ac 23). The Pharisees believed in the resurrection, and the Sadducees did not (feeling that this was only oral tradition). All Paul had to do was to hurl out that one word, and the two groups started squabbling with each other, while Paul stood to the side and watched them wrangle.

The Sadducees opposed oral tradition as well as some of the main teachings of the written Word (e.g., the resurrection), because they felt that they could not be proved directly from Moses. Since they were rationalists and also were removed from the people as aristocrats, the Sadducees lost their control of the leadership of the nation when the Temple was destroyed in 70 C.E.

MISHNAH

This brings us to a further aspect of development of mainstream Jewish life. What started in Targumim tradition as well as in further explanations of the Word and of a growing mass of tradition, was further expanded by the Pharisees, or *Tannaim*[5] scholars, of this period. Eventually, the body of tradition became known as the *Mishnah*.[6] Until 200 C.E. these traditions were carried orally. They comprise an understanding of the legal portions of the written Word of God: explanations, additions, commentaries, and other attempts to answer questions raised regarding the *Torah*.[7]

Jesus spoke of some of this tradition current in his day, saying,

> " 'BUT IN VAIN DO THEY WORSHIP ME, TEACHING AS DOC-TRINES THE PRECEPTS OF MEN.' Neglecting the command-ment of God, you hold to the tradition of men." He was also saying to them, "You nicely set aside the command-ment of God in order to keep your tradition" (Mk 7:7-9) .

Note also:

> "Invalidating the word of God by your tradition which you have handed down; and you do many things such as that" (Mk 7:13) .

What had started as a help in Ezra's day was becoming a restrictive legal influence in Jesus' day. While some tradi-

5. *Tannaim* is an Aramaic word, but in Hebrew it refers to the schol-ars who orally taught the Mishnah. At the end of the second cen-tury these religious leaders committed the Mishnah to writing.
6. *Mishnah* comes from the verb "to repeat," referring to a particular method of instruction by which the oral Law was taught with the assertion that the Scriptures support the traditions.
7. *Torah* is technically the name for the first five books of Moses, but in time it has become a word used loosely to refer to Moses' work, the rest of Scripture, and the traditions.

tion is good to help us understand Scripture, the Scripture must never take second place to the tradition.

In Ezra's day, if someone was studying to be a religious leader, he had to learn all of the Mishnah by memory. Of course, once the student obtained a grasp of this material, he was a walking Hebrew Scriptures as well as a walking Mishnah. This was Paul's background training.

By 200 C.E. much of the body of tradition was put into writing. There were several reasons for this. The Jewish people were scattered, and the religious leaders were afraid that the traditions might be lost in the Dispersion. A written tradition would aid in preserving the unity of the people. Also, there was another change in language used by the common people. In the Diaspora (Dispersion), the Jewish people were speaking Greek and Latin rather than Hebrew and Aramaic. Therefore, a Mishnah written in Hebrew by the Jewish leaders was an attempt to ensure that the Jewish people would not lose their main traditions and identity while scattered.[8]

The Mishnah is codified similarly to the Bible. There are six main divisions, and each is further divided into parts called *tractates*. There are sixty-six tractates in the entire Mishnah. Each tractate is divided into paragraphs. When we refer to any particular passage in the Mishnah, we name the tractate, chapter, and paragraph—similar to the way we refer to a passage in the Bible. The Mishnah gives us a good amount of information about practices and observations of Jewish holidays and Temple procedures in the first century C.E.

GEMARA

We move on to the next development, the period from 200-500 C.E. Here we have the *Gemara* ("completion") written in Aramaic, compiled by scholars called *Amoraim*

8. There is an English translation: Herbert Danby, *The Mishnah* (Oxford: Oxford U., 1950).

("interpreters"). The Gemara is mainly an explanation and application of the Mishnah. So, the Gemara is really a commentary on the commentary on the Scriptures. If one were to pick up a portion of the Gemara, one would find that it just goes on and on for pages, as one goes from topic to topic in following the Mishnah.

The combination of the two, the Mishnah and the Gemara, makes up the *Talmud* ("study," "learning"). When a Jewish person says, "My belief is centered in the Talmud," we know that he is speaking of the Mishnah and the Gemara. He is speaking of the commentary on the Word of God and of the commentary on the commentary of the Word of God.

When we speak of a Jerusalem Gemara, we refer to the commentary on the Mishnah worked out by the scholars in the homeland of Israel. There is a Babylonian Talmud, a commentary on the same Mishnah, worked out by the Babylonian scholars in their schools of this period.

Therefore, there are actually two Talmuds: a Jerusalem Talmud and a Babylonian Talmud. Today the most important by far is the Babylonian Talmud, for a number of reasons.[9] One of the main reasons is that the scholars in the land of Israel were persecuted periodically and did not have time to develop and write lengthy commentaries. They would write fast and then have to move from place to place. However, the Babylonian scholars were comparatively free to study, develop, and expand their work, so that the Babylonian Talmud is about three times longer than the Jerusalem Talmud. There is not much difference between the two insofar as doctrinal content is concerned, although there are some differences concerning the practices of Judaism.

The Talmud, therefore, is the rock bottom of tradition-

9. There is an English translation: Isidore Epstein, ed. and trans., *The Babylonian Talmud,* 18 vols. (London: Soncino, 1961).

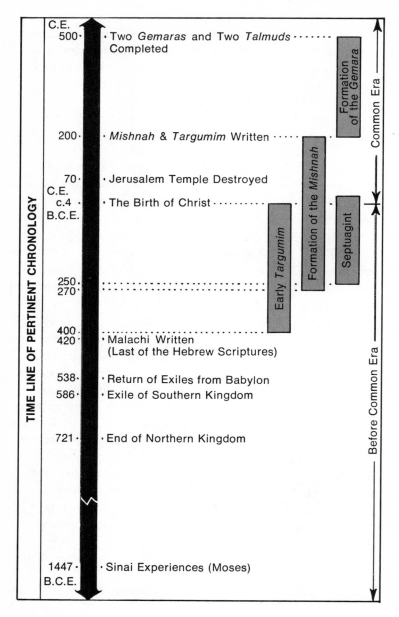

TIME LINE OF PERTINENT CHRONOLOGY

C.E.
500 · · Two *Gemaras* and Two *Talmuds* · · · · · · ·
Completed

Formation of the *Gemara*

200 · · *Mishnah* & *Targumim* Written · · · · ·

Formation of the *Mishnah*

70 · · Jerusalem Temple Destroyed
C.E.
c.4 · · The Birth of Christ · · · · · · · · ·
B.C.E.

Early *Targumim*

Septuagint

250 ·
270 ·

400 ·
420 · · Malachi Written
(Last of the Hebrew Scriptures)

538 · · Return of Exiles from Babylon
586 · · Exile of Southern Kingdom

721 · · End of Northern Kingdom

1447 · · Sinai Experiences (Moses)
B.C.E.

Common Era

Before Common Era

al, or orthodox, Judaism. This is absolutely basic. The traditional Jew looks at the Scriptures through the Talmud. He interprets Scripture by means of the insight of the Talmud. What we will say later with regard to the doctrines of Judaism will be based upon how the Talmud understands the various doctrines. For example, if we ask about the traditional belief concerning the Messiah, we must start with what the Talmud says about the concept.

CONTINUATION OF ORTHODOXY: 500-1800 C.E.

The second major phase in the development of Judaism extended from 500-1800, a period of about thirteen hundred years. It was a period of preserving the status quo insofar as a traditional Judaism was concerned. This does not mean that all the scholars were inactive. We do emphasize there was no change in the content of doctrine; however, various brilliant ways and means of expressing doctrine were developed. The energies of the scholars were spent on the methods of expressing established doctrines either through traditional Talmud study or through philosophical expression. The latter set forth in rational form the mainstream Judaism.

BABYLONIAN SCHOOLS

After 450 C.E. the center of Jewry shifted to Babylon. While we cannot treat all the leaders and scholars (i.e., the *Geonim,* or "masters" of the Babylonian schools (500-1040 C.E.) , we do take note of Saadia Gaon (d. 942) , an outstanding leader who had a tremendous intellect.

Saadia Gaon translated the Hebrew Scriptures into Arabic, and the Old Testament of one version of the Arabic Bible that we have today is due to the labors of this man. He also laid the foundation for a Jewish philosophy, and thus introduced a new note in Judaism. Saadia began the effort to express the beliefs of Judaism through the contemporary philosophy of the day. This procedure is an attempt to present systematically the characteristic beliefs of an understanding of Judaism. While this approach may have some merit, it inevitably roused the resentment of traditionalists, who felt that this was an intrusion and a device to undermine the faith of the practicing Jew.

We also need to say something, in passing, about a group of people called the Karaites. Their story is a tragedy, perhaps, in Jewish history. These people were Scripturalists. By the time 800 c.e. rolled around, mainstream Jewry had detailed instructions on every facet of life among the Jewish people. The Karaites rebelled against this and felt that they should try to break the mold and go back to the simple presentation of the Scriptures. Therein lay the dilemma. If one goes back to what only the Hebrew Scriptures had to say in 800 c.e., the traditionalists would assert that one cannot follow the strict letter of the Scriptures and that there needed to be an understanding or tradition to soften the demands of the Scripture. At the same time there was the claim by the New Testament to be the fulfillment of the Hebrew Scriptures. The New Testament asserted a relationship to the Hebrew Scriptures and declared Jesus to be the Messiah. This the Karaites would not accept. But then how did they handle the Old Testament? In time, they formed a tradition of their own and ended with a dismal note in Jewish history. Here were Scripturalists who began by rejecting orthodoxy but finished by having their own orthodoxy because they could not consider the pathway to the New Testament which a strict interpretation of the Word of God could have provided. The fortunes of the Karaites ebbed and flowed through the centuries, and there are Karaites still living today, especially in Israel.

Spanish Period

The Babylonian schools came to an end in approximately 1040 c.e.; meanwhile, the Spanish period had already begun to flourish. It is interesting to note that when one area in the Diaspora began to decline, another was prepared to take its place. The Spanish era began in 711 c.e., with the Moors' invasion of the Iberian peninsula and opened up an important period eventually known as one of the golden ages in Jewish literary production. The Jews of Spain and the Mediterranean word were *Sephardim*.

There is not enough space to mention all that was produced (see the bibliography). We note Bible exegetes like Abraham Ibn Ezra and Nahmanides. Poetry in the most elegant verse was being penned by Samuel Ibn Nagid, Solomon ibn-Gebirol, Moses Ibn Ezra, and Judah ha-Levi. If you have never read poetry by a man like Gebirol, you ought to do so. Here were expressed tremendous psalms of the heart as he cast the Hebrew Scriptures and a developed orthodoxy in unforgettable and moving poetry; some of his poety is part of the synagogue liturgy and is sung by cantors to this day. There were men who worked in philology, philosophy, and theology, such as ha-Levi, Abraham Ibn Ezra, Hasdai Crescas, and Abrabanel.

The most famous scholar of this era was Maimonides (d. 1204). He was born in Spain but accomplished most of his work in Egypt. Maimonides codified Jewish beliefs, using Aristotle as the philosophical vehicle for expressing an established orthodoxy. He is well known for his thirteen principles of faith. In sharing with a Jewish traditionalist, our challenge will be in the area of Maimonides' work, the thirteen principles of faith as well as the philosophic presentation of Judaism in his *Guide of the Perplexed*. This man is important, and his work has lasted to this day.

French Period

We also note the French period, which produced Rashi (d. 1105) and the Kimhi family (father and sons). These men were important for their interpretation of Scripture. Hardly any Jewish history books or materials on Scripture exegesis exist which do not mention these men. The commentaries of Rashi and David Kimḥi (d. 1235) guided Jewish thinking within traditional Jewish and Christian circles and continue to do so to this day. If one wants to know the orthodox interpretation of various passages of Scripture, one must examine the work of these men.

EASTERN EUROPE

There were many other leaders and scholars in Russia, Poland, and Lithuania who meant much to traditional Judaism in eastern Europe from approximately 1500 to 1800 C.E. In this period eastern Europe was the center of strength of orthodoxy as we know it today, and these Jewish people were known as *Ashkenazim*.

One phase deserves mention, and this is the movement that came as the result of the influence of Baal Shem Tov ("Master of the Good Name") in the early 1700s. He rebelled against legalistic orthodoxy but in an amiable, sweet, warmhearted way. Toward the end of the status quo period, the traditionalist was hemmed in by many rules of behavior. He was solidified in a mold of thought and practice. Orthodoxy had become cold and legal. Baal Shem Tov said, in effect, "This shouldn't be." He introduced an element in Orthodox Judaism that stressed the mystical; it was an emphasis on joy, feeling, and expression in the whole round of life. This was the start of the *Hasidim*.[10]

The traditional content of doctrine was still there, but it had a warmth of expression that touched the heart. Many became a part of this movement, and various leaders of different hasidic groups came to be known as *rebbes*. The movement has lasted to this day; and in fact, the most religious quarter in Jerusalem today is occupied by men, women, and children who are hasidim.

---

10. The Hasidim are not to be confused with the earlier *hasidim*, the religious leaders of 200-135 B.C.E.

Lack of Uniformity: 1800—Present

We come to the modern period, which some have called the period of confusion. This does not mean there is any confusion within the various groups of rabbis and religious leaders. But confusion exists in the lack of doctrine or a set of beliefs to characterize ideal Judaism. We note this when we have any kind of interaction today with Jewish people. One of the first things to determine in our sharing experience is the type of Judaism to which our Jewish acquaintance is related, if he has a religious preference.

Usually we can ask, "Where do you attend?" If they indicate a temple, we know that the reference is to a Reform place of worship. If they indicate a synagogue, we must determine whether it is Conservative or Orthodox. Beginning about 1800 c.e. we see the first break in uniformity within Judaism. Leading the way was Reform Judaism, which originated in Europe.

Reform Judaism in Europe

A number of factors contributed to the origin of Reform Judaism (see chap. 2). Reform Judaism emerged because there was a change in attitude on the part of many Europeans toward Jewish people. The French Revolution, for example, did much to release the Jewish people from the status of second-class citizenship. The Austrian Edict of Toleration in 1782 by Joseph II stated, "To me the Jews are human beings, consumers and tax payers and consequently useful if properly kept in check."[11] Today we would regard his words with disdain and dismay, but in 1782 words like these were a bright spotlight.

Moses Mendelssohn (d. 1786) may be considered the father of Reform Judaism. In his objectives he sought to relate Jewish people with western European culture. He

11. Richard Steinbrink, "Reform Judaism," in *Currents and Trends in Contemporary Jewish Thought,* ed. Benjamin Efron (New York: Ktav, 1965), p. 34.

called on his fellow Jews to be "rational in faith, orthodox in practice and German in culture."[12] This is difficult to comprehend. To be rational, Orthodox Jewish, and culturally German at the same time is a tall order. But note Mendelssohn's purposes: he was trying to lead Jewish people out of the ghettos and into the mainstream of western European cultural life. This was his life's work. A number of leaders who followed after Mendelssohn pared down the beliefs of traditional Judaism and made it possible for the Jew, if he so desired, to live in the midst of Western culture.

Note also the dismal ultimate results of Reform Judaism. In its cultural and rational ties, it contained the seeds of its own destruction. Reform Jewish leaders came under the influence of the higher criticism of Scripture, which attacked the integrity of the Word of God.[13] A prolonged attack on the inerrancy of the Word of God in the West eventually spawned a generation which did not respect the Scriptures. Hand in glove with this went lack of respect for the Jew. And in the long run, where did it all lead? In Germany, for example, it led to the persecution of the Jew and ultimately to the "solution to the Jewish problem": racial genocide. It took over a century for the procedure to run its course—with disastrous results.

REFORM JUDAISM IN AMERICA

Reform Judaism came to America when large numbers of German Jews emigrated to the United States between 1840 and 1870, settling mainly in the Midwest. Today Reform Judaism, following most of the principles laid down in Germany, is located in major cities in the United States. Since the birth of the state of Israel, Reform Juda-

12. Ibid., p. 35.
13. For a further discussion of higher criticism, see William E. Hordern, *Layman's Guide to Protestant Theology*, rev. ed., (New York: Macmillan, 1968), pp. 41-50.

ism has been having some second thoughts about its original objectives; some are once more considering a measured turn to a more conservative stand.

CONSERVATIVE JUDAISM

The third movement, Conservative Judaism, is a distinctively American product, although it had its roots in Germany in the work of Zechariah Frankel (d. 1875).

This movement developed among immigrants from Europe. Many eastern European Jews, suffering extreme persecution, emigrated to the United States toward the end of the nineteenth century and in the first two decades of this century. The first generation adhered to the traditional Judaism they brought with them. German Reform Judaism made few inroads into this traditional religious expression. On the other hand, a second generation of eastern European folk did not want to be confined to the orthodoxy of the first generation. The American way of life, schooling, training, social advantages, and economic opportunities did much to break down the ghetto outlook of strict orthodoxy.

The Jewish religious leaders had to make a decision. Reform Judaism was not appealing, because it threw away too much and became critical of the Scriptures and traditions. Traditionalism was too strict. A third group was born, a group that stood between Reform and Orthodoxy. The new group held to the doctrinal beliefs of traditional Judaism, but in practice it sought to adapt as much as possible to the American way of life.

In the United States today we have traditional Judaism, Reform Judaism, and Conservative Judaism. Some have described the situation as confusion, because there is no uniform belief accepted by all of Judaism. There are many different opinions and many different expressions of beliefs.

ORTHODOXY, RECONSTRUCTION, AND AGNOSTICISM

Since 1948, the presence of the State of Israel has caused traditionalism to have a slight resurgence of life in America. Reform Judaism has halted in its tracks because of the diversity of opinions in its ranks regarding Israel. Most Jewish people today are in the conservative wing.

There is also a reconstructionism. It is highly complex, combining some basics of Judaism and elements of the modern scientific outlook. Judaism becomes a kind of folk religion that Jewish people had developed across the centuries. God is regarded as a cosmic process at work among people to give them individual worth and social consciousness. This obviously is no longer the concept of God as the Supreme Being who has created the universe and with whom man can have a personal relationship. Even though some of the leaders are well educated and highly articulate, reconstructionism attracts only a few Jewish people. One rarely encounters a reconstructionist Jew.

One sees many agnostics among Jewish people in this country—especially among the young people on our college campuses. They do not follow any particular group, and it is among them that one senses an extreme spiritual hunger.

RELIGION IN ISRAEL

In Israel, the only recognized religious party is the traditional, but it includes a wide gamut of expression. Other religious groups are present, but they are not recognized as political parties. Only about 40 percent of the population practice Judaism with any regularity. More than half of the people are agnostic. All in the public schools study the Hebrew Scriptures, but more than half neither deny nor affirm traditional Jewish beliefs. Many are struggling in an attempt to make the Scriptures relevant for twentieth-century needs, indicating that traditionalism does not do this. This is an interesting struggle to watch, for God is at work with hearts so that consideration can be given to the claims of the whole Word of God. (See chap. 11 for further information on the religious situation in Israel.)

FOR FURTHER STUDY

BOOKS

Epstein, I. *Judaism*. Baltimore: Penguin, 1959. This study from the Jewish point of view is by a prolific author who edited the Soncino edition of the Babylonian Talmud.

Finkelstein, Louis. *The Jews: Their History, Culture, and Religion*. 2 vols. New York: Harper, 1949. For years the author was president of the Jewish Theological Seminary of America in New York.

Graetz, H. *History of the Jews*. 6 vols. Philadelphia: Jewish Publ. Soc. of America, 1939. The only drawback of this classic history of the Jewish people is that it does not go beyond the nineteenth century.

Grayzel, S. *History of the Jews*. 6 vols. Philadelphia: Jewish Publ. Soc. of America, 1952. This is a concise, one-volume presentation.

———. *A History of the Contemporary Jews*. New York: Harper, 1960. This work concerning Jewish people of this century is a companion to his other concise volume.

Hull, W. *The Fall and Rise of Israel*. Grand Rapids: Zondervan, 1954. The author served the Lord in the Holy Land for years.

Parkes, James. *A History of the Jewish People*. Baltimore: Penguin, 1964. This English author has given his life to the study of Jewish people and their history.

FILMSTRIPS

National Council on Jewish Audio-Visual Materials. *Jewish Life in Palestine and Babylonia*. New York: Amer. Assoc. for Jewish Ed.

Tadmor, Shlomo, researcher. Land of Israel series (see individual titles below). New Rochelle, N.Y.: Pathescope Ed. Films.

1-4. *Complete Overview History of the Land of Israel*
15. *A More Detailed Description of the Hellenistic and Maccabean Period*
16. *A More Detailed Description of the Roman Period*
17. *A More Detailed Description of the Roman Period to the Present*

These may be obtained from Pathescope Educational Films, Inc., 71 Weyman Avenue, New Rochelle, New York 10802.

2

THE JEWISH PEOPLE AND THE CHURCH

INTRODUCTION

One of the tragedies of history is the relationship between the Jewish people and the Church. The Church, which was once Jewish, became, in many instances, so anti-Jewish that one wonders if time was ever taken to see the Jewishness of the Saviour, the Jewishness of the gospels and parts of the New Testament, and the fact that Gentile believers in the Saviour are spiritual sons of Abraham (Gal 3:29).

We introduce this tragedy in relationships because as Christians we need to understand the difficulties this causes in sharing our faith with our Jewish friends. And, as we learn more of the story of this relationship, we can have a more sympathetic grasp of the attitude of the Jewish person when he meets us. Most Christians know little of Jewish history from the end of the New Testament to 1948, which marks the birth of the state of Israel. Jewish people remember too keenly the injustices they suffered at the hands of Christendom. For this reason most make no effort to consider the distinction between those who are genuine Christians and have a love for Jewish people, and those who are not born again.

FIRST CENTURY

MESSIANIC JEWS AMIDST ISRAEL

We recognize that in the first century most believers in

27

Jesus the Messiah were Jewish. This is an important point
to make when sharing with our Jewish friends. Christianity
in its New Testament expression should not be foreign to
the Jewish mind.[1] That it became so is due to the life, beliefs, and practices of a predominantly Gentile Church in
subsequent centuries. But in the beginning most believers
were Messianic Jews.[2] When we see New Testament names
like Jesus, Paul, Peter, James, and John, in their Hebrew
equivalents—Yeshua, Sha'ul, Shimon, Yaacov, and Yoḥa-
nan—we should recognize the Jewishness of these men
and not rob them or other Messianic Jews of their identity.[3] When we study the content of the New Testament that pertains to the land of Israel, we see the Jewishness of the background. The first believers lived among
their *brethren* and shared the message that Jesus is the
Messiah. These Messianic Jews indicated to their own
flesh and blood that Jesus fulfilled the Messianic message
of the Old Testament and stood ready to fulfill the Kingdom promises. And these witnesses were successful in their
attempts when, as some have estimated, at least one-fourth
of the nation responded to the message by the end of the
first century c.e. A great number of priests also became
Messianic Jews (Ac 6:7).

1. The New Testament is a major source of information about Jewish
   culture, activities, and beliefs in the first century c.e. and is studied
   in universities in Israel. A life of Jesus from the gospels of Matthew,
   Mark, and Luke is presented in the junior high schools.
2. *Messianic Jew* is the name that describes a Jewish person who has
   acknowledged Jesus as his Messiah and his atonement for sin and
   affirms his ethnic identity with Jewish people. This is discussed in
   chaps. 9 and 11.
3. Many object that this raises again the barrier between Jewish believers and Gentile believers in the Church and is contrary to Gal
   3:28: "There is neither Jew nor Greek, . . . for you are all one in
   Christ Jesus." The Messianic Jew readily agrees that *spiritually* speaking the Jewish believer and the Gentile believer are one in the body
   of the Messiah; however, humanly and ethnically speaking, there
   are differences—as the scripture passage goes on to stress so elo-
   quently. For purposes of faith sharing, we never take away the ethnic identity of our Jewish friend—even as Paul emphasized in 1 Co
   9:20.

MESSIANIC JEWS SHARE WITH GENTILES

With prodding, these Jewish believers also confronted Gentiles with the Gospel message. The use of the word *prodding* is not to disparage anyone; it is just in recognition of human nature. From our own experience, we know the tendency to fellowship only with our own circle and not to move out unless God does something to push us out. The Jewish believers were no different. The New Testament describes how God providentially scattered the believers that they should witness (Ac 8:4). Consider also the problems in Paul's ministry (Ac 9:15-16) as he went out to preach the message of Jesus the Redeemer from sin, and churches were founded as a result. We note, as we read the last chapter of most of his books, that many of Paul's companions were Messianic Jews. Many of the Jewish believers in the first century founded the churches, which were made up of Jewish believers and many Gentile proselytes. The first century witnessed some of the finest efforts for God by Messianic Jews.

SECOND AND THIRD CENTURIES

CHANGE IN THE NATURE OF THE CHURCH

In the second and third centuries, the Church began to become more and more Gentile. In the face of its universal appeal, this was inevitable. There were more Gentiles than Jews, and the Church began to assume a universal composite. However, the Church still included a great number of Messianic Jews. Because of pressure by the Roman government on Israel, the relationship between Jewish people and the Church (Jewish and Gentile believers) was often good.[4]

4. We must never forget a providential situation in the first-century world. Messianic Jews founded churches all over the Mediterranean world prior to the destruction of the Temple in 70 C.E. After the destruction of the Temple, many Jewish people fled across the Mediterranean world and were confronted by Jewish and Gentile believers who explained to the Jewish refugees the significance of this new exile. In this time of calamity, no doubt many Jewish people responded to the New Testament message, which emphasized the grace and love of God for His people Israel.

CHURCH DIALOGUE WITH ISRAEL

One of the most famous of the Church's dialogues with Israel was Justin Martyr's *Dialogue with Trypho, a Jew,* in which Justin Martyr sought to prove the Messiahship of Jesus and also discussed the place of the Law within the New Testament context. He complained of mistreatment of Jewish believers in Jesus as Messiah by some of the Jewish religious leaders; nevertheless, he was peaceful and courteous toward the Jewish people. As a rule, he showed a concern for them.

In one of the early documents, the Didascalia, Christians were enjoined to pray for Jewish people during the Passover. Jewish people were to be called brothers—not in the Spirit, because there was a recognition that they needed to be born again, but in a fraternal sense. There was an attempt on the part of many in the Church to reach out and touch the hearts and lives of Jewish people.

This was also the period when scholars were thinking through New Testament doctrine. Some of this doctrine did not agree with the developing Judaism (see chap. 1), but we make a distinction between disagreement and anti-Jewishness. We may not agree with some Jewish beliefs, but this is certainly no excuse to dislike the Jew. We can share our own beliefs and do it in a sweet-spirited way so as to be good ambassadors of Jesus, who, in the days of His flesh, chose to be a Jew within the household of Israel.

A HOSTILE NOTE

However, there were ominous rumblings within the Church. Some churchmen were impatient with Jewish people and were expressing hostility. "They [Jews] will always be slaves. For their past sins, they have found pardon, but are now to be left desolate because they killed the son of their benefactor" were the words of Hippolytus in *Demonstratio Adversus Judaeos,* as he commented on a line from Psalm 69.

FOURTH CENTURY

CHRISTIANITY—A STATE RELIGION

In the fourth century, Christianity became a state-sanctioned religion. With Constantine's adherence to Christianity, the Church was recognized and was never persecuted by the Roman government again (except under Julian the Apostate, although his reign lasted only from 360 to 363 C.E.). Christianity was made official. But it also became necessary to be a member of a church in order to advance politically in the Roman government. It is obvious what would happen. Prior to this, persecutions had largely kept the Church pure, but now the Church became flooded with nonbelievers.

DETERIORATION OF JEWISH IMAGE AND STATUS

A number of factors now contributed to the deterioration of the Jewish image and status. Certainly, the new composition of the Church aided in the breakdown of relations with Jewish people. Nonbelievers, as members of churches, brought their prejudices and their anti-Jewishness with them into the church;[5] and this began to rupture any productive relations between the mother and daughter beliefs. In addition to the previously mentioned Hippolytus, other church leaders added to the breakdown. Cyprian, in his *Ad Quirinum* (in which he propounded a detailed refutation of Judaism) and in his *Contra Celsus,* stated, "They [Jews] will never be restored to their former condition. For they committed a crime of the most unhallowed kind, in conspiring against the Saviour of the human race."[6] This added grist to the mill grinding out latent anti-Jewish sentiment. Scripture was interpreted in a way to take advantage

5. The word *church* is used here in the broadest sense. To be sure, there could have been many local churches which were not affected in this manner.
6. As quoted by Edward Flannery, *Anguish of the Jews: Twenty-Three Centuries of Anti-Semitism* (New York: Macmillan, 1965), p. 38.

of every unflattering reference to Jewish people, especially in the Hebrew Scriptures. There was a growing emphasis on Jewish miseries as the result of divine punishment for the crucifixion of Christ. All of this contributed to the loss of any positive image of Jews in the eyes of people and laid the groundwork for the deicide charge that was to last for centuries.

THE NEW TESTAMENT APOLOGISTS: ANTI-JEWISH ATTITUDE

We have already mentioned a number of divisive leaders in the Church-Jewish relationship. While the apologies for the doctrines of the New Testament cannot be considered totally anti-Jewish, nevertheless, a groundwork was laid for what was to come.[7]

Eventually we come to Chrysostom (d. 407). He was regarded as one of the greatest preachers of the early Church and wrote a number of grand homilies which have been studied through the centuries with great spiritual profit. However, the homilies are anything but epistles of love for the Jewish people. A few quotations will suffice for our purposes:

> How can Christians dare "have the slightest converse" with Jews, "most miserable of all men" (4:1).

> Why are Jews degenerate? Because of their "odious assassination of Christ" (6:4) . . . there is "no expiation possible" . . . (6:2).

> The rejection and dispersion of the Jews was the work of God, not the emperors: "It was done by the wrath of God and His absolute abandon of you" (6:4).

---

7. Please note carefully that we are speaking of the apologetics of these divisive church leaders. In no way, as some have asserted, is there anti-Jewishness in the New Testament itself. One need only know the historical and cultural background and the men who wrote the New Testament to refute such a charge concerning the New Testament.

It is the duty of Christians to hate the Jews: "He who can never love Christ enough will never have done fighting against those [Jews] who hate Him" (7:1).

The Synagogue . . . is . . . a "house of prostitution" . . . (6:5), a place of "shame and ridicule" (1:3), "the domicile of the devil" (1:6), . . . "an assembly of criminals" (1:2).[8]

These are only a few vitriolic statements drawn from a great number, and they were preached from the pulpits. With men like Chrysostom, Gregory of Nyssa, Cyril of Jersualem, and even Jerome making such statements from pulpits, we can understand the effect this irresponsibility had. It opened the door for a flood tide of anti-Jewishness. There is evidence that toward the end of Chrysostom's life he was sorry for what he had said, but it was too late. The damage was done. Hate was sown in the hearts and lives of people and bore evil fruit as it passed from generation to generation, even to this day.

We see some of its effect on Augustine. In his evaluation of Jewish-Church relations, he had two views. He was faithful to the teaching of Paul that the Church should have a loving concern for Jewish people. With respect to him, we have to indicate that he stressed this in his writings.

But there was another side to Augustine. He tried to solve the problem of the survival of the Jews as a people and yet at the same time explain their misfortune. He expounded his "theology of the witness people" in which he emphasized that the Jewish people were like Cain, having a divine mark on them. They were to be an example to the Gentile people and the Church. As we see them marked, he declared, we ought to consider the divine judgment of them for rejecting Christ and thus receive Christ ourselves, noting the fearful consequences of not doing so. Upon seeing the Jewish people, Gentiles would realize that God had

8. Flannery, pp. 48-49.

set aside the Jewish people and be reminded of God's favor for the Gentiles.

The tragedy is that too many people forget or do not mention Augustine's teaching that enjoined a love for the Jewish people, but rather they remember his concept that the Jew is some kind of detestable sign. This detracts from even regarding Jewish people as human beings and recognizing that they, too, have human dignity.

Fifth Century: Total Rupture in Jewish-Church Relations

The fifth century saw a tragic break. By the middle of the century, the rupture in Jewish-Church relations was complete. The Jew was regarded as a guilt-laden unbeliever, resistant to grace and destructive to souls. This, by and large, was the Church's assessment of the Jew. Furthermore, church theology guided the empire; and while the Jew might be protected as a second-rate citizen, he was not respected for what he was or believed. The Jewish patriarchate in Israel ended in 425 c.e. The Byzantine (Eastern) church built churches all over Israel and in general was the custodian there until the Arabs came in 640 c.e.

Fifth to Nineteenth Centuries

Fortunes of Jewish People in General

From the fifth to the nineteenth centuries, Jewish people experienced reprehensible conditions in countries within Christendom. The tragedy is that the Jew fared better in non-Christian situations than under the Church in this period. Was this some quirk of cruel circumstances? As a rule, non-Christians had more of a regard for the Jew than those who called themselves Christians. In Spain Jewish people had more privileges under the Muslim than they did under the Church. The Jews were better off in the Persian Empire at the hands of nonbelievers than they were in the land of Israel under the Byzantine influence. This is not to say there were not Christians and churches here and there who effected an understanding with Jewish people; but the Church as an institution in this period was not known for its love for Jewish people.

Our attention is directed to the Roman Catholic priest Father Flannery, who in his book, *The Anguish of the Jews,* presents a thorough, scholarly study of anti-Jewish sentiment. His opinion is that the period extending from 1000 to 1500 A.D. was a vale of tears for the Jewish people. He calls it a "scandal of Christian history" that while the Church and the Christian state were at the peak of their power and influence, the sons of Israel reached the depths of affliction.[9] This period included some of the darkest pages of Jewish history. Flannery observes that in 1000 the situation of the Jewish people was fairly stable; in 1200, the Jewish people were almost paupers; by 1300, the Jewish people were terrorized.[10]

Is it any wonder that, while I was growing up, my father spoke disparagingly of those who were supposed to represent Jesus Christ? Do we not see the barrier that Christians must overcome in order to share with Jewish people their faith concerning Jesus as Messiah and Redeemer? We have to hurdle the barrier of hundreds of years of persecution and oppression at the hands of an institutional church.

ANTI-JEWISH THRUSTS

What were the immediate incidents that expressed this anti-Jewishness? First, there were the Crusades. The first crusade was a horror for Jewish people in Europe. The Church called for a crusade of soldiers who were "Christian" to go to the Holy Land to rid it of the unbelievers, the infidels. However, as they were marching to the ports of southern Europe to take passage to the East, they said,

9. Ibid., p. 89.
10. Ibid, pp. 89-90.

> We desire to combat the enemies of God in the east, but
> we have under our eyes the Jew, a race more inimical to
> God than all the others. We are doing this whole thing
> backward. First get rid of the Jew.[11]

So they presented the Jew with a choice: baptism or death.
Many chose the latter. To their credit, a number of leaders
in the Church tried to stop the senseless actions of the mobs.

There was also the charge of ritual murder. This was a
horrible insinuation that was widely believed among many
of the common people. Every time the Passover came
around, a rumor would be circulated that some Jewish person had killed a Christian child and appropriated the blood
for Passover usage. This charge of murder and cannibalism
sounds unbelievable in our day. However, with a report
like this circulating, mobs would be set free to rummage
and pillage synagogues and frighten and kill Jewish folk by
the hundreds. Many popes did attempt to exonerate Jewish
people from these charges, but not until modern times was
the falsity of all such charges of ritual murder finally and
completely established. In spite of well-meaning efforts
of some leaders, it was almost impossible to strip away the
conception of the satanic guise of the Jew often held by
the secular clergy and lay people of the Church in general.

Then, of course, there was the abominable distinctive
badge or article of clothing. So-called Christian govern-
ments required Jews to wear badges or distinctive dress to
mark them as Jews. To say the least, it was degrading and
demoralizing.

The Black Death of Europe was the name given to the
devastating plague that struck Europe in 1347-50. According to conservative estimates, one-fourth of Europe's population died in this scourge. Because of their practice of the
basic rules of hygiene, Jewish people as a whole were not
as subject to the plague as others of the common people.

11. Gilbert of Nogent *De Vita Sua* 3.5, as cited by Flannery, *Anguish of
the Jews*, p. 90.

But superstitious mobs, not understanding this, believed that the Jewish people were responsible for the plague and accused them of causing it by poisoning the wells. Mobs, given free reign, vented their wrath against Jewish people and killed countless numbers.

Compulsory periodic attendance at preaching services was another form of degradation. Beginning in the thirteenth century, the Dominicans and Franciscans forced the Jewish people to sit for an hour, two hours, sometimes three hours at a time to listen to sermons, with the idea of making them believe the doctrines of the Roman church. Sometimes listeners were even examined for cotton in their ears to make sure that they heard the preaching. Many did become believers, but it was a wonder with this kind of practice. The preachers felt they were serving God in following a literal interpretation of compelling Jews to come to Christ (Lk 14:23) . This practice did not cease in many places until 1848.

Ferdinand and Isabella and the Spanish Edict of Expulsion were the summit of ignominy in the Jewish period in Spain. We learn in school that in 1492 Columbus sailed the ocean blue, and that Ferdinand and Isabella went through great pains to raise the money to send Columbus on his voyage. The truth of the matter is that in 1492, after all the Moors had been driven out of Spain, Jewish people were given only a few short months to leave Spain. Jewish possessions were sold for a song, and property was confiscated by the government (unless the Jews converted and were baptized into the church) . On this occasion, most chose to exit rather than submit. Consequently, many died, and the few who were left fled across Europe or to the eastern Mediterranean, which was under Turkish domination. To this day, Christianity is seen by many Jews in terms of the church's actions in the Spain of 1492.

The ghetto was another example of deprivation of human dignity. Every major city in Europe had a ghetto, which was a small, restricted area where the Jews were to live. Some Jews could leave it to transact business, but this was the area where the Jews were mainly confined. The idea was that Christians should be kept from contact with Jewish people. Ironically, it was not through the church's efforts that Jewish folk began to be released from the ghettos. The French Revolution and secular humanitarians advocated greater freedom of all individuals. The Jews began to come out of the ghettos in the early nineteenth century and take part in Western life as a result of a humanitarianism based on a secular rationalism. However, the ghetto did have a positive effect through the centuries in keeping Jewish people together and preserving their unity and religious practices.

REFORMATION

The Reformation brought a renewed emphasis on the great doctrines of the Word of God, for example, the priority of Scripture and justification by faith. In the beginning of his ministry, Luther was kindly disposed toward the Jewish people. He studied Hebrew under the great Hebraist Reuchlin, and Luther's ability to translate the Scriptures from Hebrew into German is a tribute to the work of producing a Bible in the vernacular of his people. However, toward the end of his life, Luther had hardly a kind word to say about the Jews; although, to be fair to him, his relationships with all people were difficult in his last years.

It is to the credit of the Lutheran church that there was always an element that did not let Luther's last words about the Jews affect them, but they sought to share their faith with Jewish people. In the 1700s fruitful efforts were mainly by the pietists, and during the nineteenth century the Lutheran church had many Jewish believers in its ranks.

The Reformed church had its influence on the churches

in Holland and among the Presbyterians. The church in Holland made that country a haven for Jewish people, and the Presbyterian church also shared its faith in many ways with them.

Eastern Europe

The experience in eastern Europe was most heartrending. Among the greatest slaughters of Jewish people in history were the Chmielnicki massacre of 1648 and those which followed in that decade. The actual number of those killed is not known, but it has been estimated anywhere from a hundred thousand to one-half million. These people were murdered within a few years. Whole Jewish communities were destroyed, and to this century the major countries of eastern Europe have never been kindly disposed toward the Jewish people.

Eventually, the conditions resulted in a mass migration to America. The estimate is that at least seven-hundred-fifty thousand Jewish people emigrated to the United States in the period between 1880 and World War I. The Jewish people of this period also emigrated from eastern Europe to Israel, and many of the Israeli settlers in the 1870s and 1880s came from Russia and Poland. Some of the early settlers were instrumental in laying the foundations of the state of Israel.

Eighteenth Century to the Present

Torturous Path to Emancipation

The Jew found that the road to emancipation was long and torturous. In many areas, there still is not complete freedom for the Jew to practice his faith openly. In chapter 1 a few milestones in the long, difficult struggle for increased dignity during the eighteenth century were mentioned—for examples, the Austrian Edict and the German Reform movement. The French Revolution had its part

as well as the social revolutions in Europe during the 1800s.
But advance was slow. For example, even Baron Lionel
Rothschild had to return five times to the English Parlia-
ment before he was allowed to vote in the mid-1800s. Economic, social, and educational deprivations continued well
into the twentieth century and have only begun to be rectified in this country since World War II. It was the holocaust[12] of the twentieth century that finally awakened the
conscience of the church and forced a reevaluation of the
whole Jewish-Church relationship. It is to be hoped that
this interest, because of a frightful cost in human life, will
not be lost in shallow thinking and feeling.

DANGERS OF THE EMANCIPATION

Emancipation does not solve all problems, however. Beginning with the Reform in Germany and eventually in the
rest of the Western countries, the Jewish person began to
experience greater freedom to live. He could enter into the
culture of the country in which he resided and practice or
not practice his faith as he chose. While this enhanced the
Jewish person's opportunity to formulate his own world-
view, a question can be raised as to what happens to the
identity of the Jew. In Germany, the Jew assimilated almost to the point where there would hardly have been a
Jewish identity but for the rise of National Socialism. The
situation in the United States is proceeding today in the
same pattern. Jewish sociologists indicate that at the present rate of assimilation half of the United States' population
of Jewry—almost three million—may be well-nigh lost by
the year 2000. Although emancipation does raise the dignity of the Jewish person, it also carries the danger of loss
of identity.

On the other hand, there is more opportunity than ever

12. *Holocaust* refers to the death of six million Jews at the hands of the
German National Socialist regime as the final attempt at a solution
to the "Jewish problem."

for good Jewish-Church relations. The emancipation should allow the Jewish person and Christian to understand each other and share in mutual concerns. At the same time the Christian may share his faith in Israel's Messiah with the Jew. For the Church to do any less would be a serious dereliction of responsibility.

CONCLUSION

We have already indicated that the rupture of Jewish-Church relations took place in the fourth and fifth centuries. In the eighteenth and nineteenth centuries, we see a rebirth of the Church's interest in befriending the Jew. With the improvement of relationships the Christian can share his faith to win the Jewish person to the Messiah. We have already pointed out some sections of the Lutheran church in Germany that felt the responsibility for faith sharing and won many Jewish people in the nineteenth century. The nineteenth century also saw the birth of many evangelistic societies in England which sent their workers across the European continent. Through the efforts of these folk, many Jewish people became Messianic Jews.

The nineteenth century saw a *recorded* two hundred fifty thousand Jewish people come to the Lord. No doubt, there were many, many more. However, the work of the societies in Britain and North America in the first half of the twentieth century has already resulted in more coming to the Lord than in all of the nineteenth century. And in the last half of this century, the response continues at an unprecedented pace. The combined efforts of the societies and individual churches that have befriended Jewish people have an unparalleled privilege of establishing and enhancing relations with Jewish people. The spiritual hunger today provides a tremendous opportunity to proclaim the One who can satisfy the craving of the human heart.

FOR FURTHER STUDY

BOOKS

Eckardt, Alice, and Eckardt, Roy. *Encounter with Israel.* New York: Association Press, 1970. Writing from the liberal theological perspective, the Eckardts have nevertheless made Jewish history and culture their specialty and have much to offer to Christians.

Flannery, Edward. *The Anguish of the Jews.* New York: Macmillan, 1965. Flannery provides an excellent, scholarly study of anti-Semitism through the centuries.

Hull, William. *The Fall and Rise of Israel.* Grand Rapids: Zondervan, 1954. Hull has emphasized the problems of the birth of the state of Israel.

Parkes, James. *The Conflict of the Church and the Synagogue.* Philadelphia: Jewish Publ. Soc. of Amer., 1964.

FILMSTRIPS

National Council on Jewish Audio-Visual Materials. *Jewish Life in the Middle Ages.* New York: Amer. Assoc. for Jewish Ed.

FILMS

Let My People Go. New York: Xerox. This film is distributed by the Jim Handy Organization, New York, N.Y.

3

JEWISH HOLIDAYS

INTRODUCTION

For the Jewish person who practices at least some form of Judaism, life is ordered by the Jewish religious calendar all year long. We should be acquainted with this so that our Jewish friends can sense our genuine desire to be sympathetic and understanding. The Jewish holidays also provide rich meaning in understanding the New Testament.

Jewish people have two calendars, reflecting a sacred and a civil year. The religious year begins with the month *Nisan* (March-April) and the civil year with the month *Tishri* (September-October). The first month of the civil calendar is the seventh month of the religious calendar.

Traditional Jews and Conservative Jews observe the religious calendar, with the former being more meticulous in their practice. Reform Jews have modified and minimized much of the practice of the observances, and many keep only enough of the practice to insure some kind of identity.[1]

PASSOVER

GENERAL

First on the religious calendar of festivals is the observance of redemption, Passover (Pesaḥ), the oldest of Jewish

---

1. The descriptions of the observance of the holidays are given in some detail in this chapter. However, it is the Traditional Jewish person who observes all that are mentioned. Others are less meticulous in their practice of Judaism.

43

festivals. It is a spring festival (March-April), beginning on the eve of the fourteenth day of Nisan.[2] It now lasts eight days, although originally it lasted seven days. It is coincident with Good Friday and Easter, and is significant in this respect. Its biblical basis is found in Exodus 12:1-50; 13:1-10; Leviticus 23:5-8; Numbers 9:1-14; 28:16-25; Deuteronomy 16:1-8. During the course of the centuries its observance has changed. The most important change is the absence of the sacrificial lamb since the destruction of the second Temple. The modern Passover is therefore not a biblical Passover at all, because the roast lamb is missing.

The word *pesah* means "to pass over." This festival is so named because the angel of God passed over the dwellings of the Hebrews wherever the blood of the Passover lamb was sprinkled on the doorposts on the night when the angel slew the firstborn of every Egyptian family. It commemorates the redemption from Egypt. It is characterized chiefly today by eating unleavened bread, *masah* during the entire period of the festival and by the absence of all leaven, *hames*.

IN THE HOME

The main celebration of this festival is in the home, and it is the privilege of the father of a family or the patriarch of the clan to lead in the observance of Passover.

Searching for the Leaven. A ceremonial search for leaven is made the night before the eve of Pesah. Every nook and cranny is searched to be sure no leaven is present. Leaven has already been placed in certain places so that the blessing to be uttered on finding it is not said in vain. It is burned the next morning in a ceremony called the burning of the leaven.

Since the word *hames* has a wide application and means anything that may undergo process of fermentation as well

2. The Jewish calendar is a lunar calendar and is quite complicated. Because of its differences with the solar calendar, the Passover date can vary from March 26 to April 25.

as anything touched by leaven, this ceremony means a great deal of household preparation and cleaning, the putting away of most ordinary food, and the use of a different set of pots, pans, and dishes kept especially for Pesaḥ. Orthodox Jews and Conservative Jews are meticulous in observance in this respect.

Seder. The outstanding ceremony in the home is the *Seder,* which means "order of service." It is observed on the first two nights of the Passover after the evening service in the synagogue. The Seder is based on a feast in which the slavery in and redemption from Egypt are symbolized by various objects. There is also the reading of the *Haggadah* ("telling," "story") throughout the ceremony and meal. It contains the story of Egypt embellished with much tradition and lore, and forms the basis for the *Seder.*[3]

Four cups of wine are taken during the dinner. An extra cup and chair are placed for Elijah, for it is generally expected that during Pesaḥ Messiah will come with Elijah as His herald. At a certain time in the ceremony the door is opened for Elijah. A benediction is then uttered, "Blessed is he who cometh," as well as prayer based on Psalms 79:6; 69:25; Lamentations 3:66. It was the third cup after the Last Supper (which was a Passover meal) that Jesus of Nazareth used to institute the cup of the communion table.

Three maṣot are wrapped in a white linen napkin. At a certain time, the middle one of these is broken in half; and one half, the *afikomen,* is hidden.[4] It is brought out at the close of the meal and is the last food to be eaten. This

---

3. One current haggadah is *Haggadah for the American Family* by Martin Berkowitz (Miami: Sacred Press, 1958).
4. The children at the table try to find this hidden piece before the seder comes to an end. The one who finds it receives a present. Some have seen in the pieces of maṣah a symbolism of the complex nature of God. The three pieces of unleavened bread represent the persons of the Godhead, and it is the middle piece that is broken. Note even the symbolism of the children who find the broken piece and receive a gift. When one finds the Messiah, second Person of the Godhead, he receives eternal life (Ro 6:23).

was the bread that Jesus of Nazareth used to institute the bread of the communion table.

There are other items on the table. There is the shank bone of a lamb, a memorial of the Passover Lamb. Prior to the destruction of the Temple, the main meat was the roasted lamb. The shank bone today is mute testimony of the missing Temple. A roasted egg is on the table also, as an emblem of mourning, inasmuch as the joys of the Temple service can no longer be experienced. The egg was not part of the seder prior to the destruction of the Temple. *Haroset,* which is a mixture of minced apples, ground almonds, spices, cinnamon, and wine, represents the mortar with which the Hebrews worked in Pharoah's building projects. Bitter herbs are there also, reminding one of the bitter bondage. Parsley dipped in salt water also speaks of the bondage in which work was performed in Egypt.

Another custom is singing the Hallel, which combines Psalms 113-118 in separate sequences, during the evening. The Seder represents a time of joy and freedom. The people around the table recline during the entire service and meal as a symbol of freedom and ease. The youngest of the family asks the traditional four questions: Why maṣot? Why bitters? Why dip twice? Why recline on pillows?

In the Synagogue

A festive spirit prevails in the synagogue. Special portions read from the prophets are Ezekiel 37:1-14; Isaiah 10:32; 12:6. At the close of the service a song called Ḥad Gadya, symbolizing Israel's sufferings and deliverances from various oppressors during her long history, is sung.

Counting of the Omer

After the service of the eve of the second day of Pesaḥ the counting of the 'omer, called sᵉfirah, begins.[5] It con-

5. This 'omer ("sheaf") refers to the sheaf of the firstfruits which the Israelites were commanded to offer in the sanctuary on the second day of Passover.

tinues for seven weeks, until the day after the seven weeks, the fiftieth day—hence the term *Pentecost* (Gk., "fiftieth day"), or the Jewish *shavuot* ("weeks"). One sees immediately the tie between the Jewish religious calendar and the Church calendar.

On the first day of the counting, the offering of the first-fruits of the first harvest (barley) is brought. In ancient times the *ḥagigah,* a festive sacrifice, was also offered.

NEW TESTAMENT PARALLELS AND SPIRITUAL SIGNIFICANCE

The Passover sets for the lamb and its shed blood as grounds and means of God's salvation for mankind (Is 53: 5-6). The pascal lamb is one of the most exacting types in Scripture of the Lamb of God (Jn 1:29). The lamb slain in faith (and the blood sprinkled in token of dependence on God for deliverance) was to be assurance for the believer (Ex 12:8-9). The bitter herbs are symbolic not only of the bitterness of past afflictions but also of sorrow for sin and the trials and conflicts of the faithful.

In 1 Corinthians 5:7-8 the apostle refers to the searching for leaven already indicated. However, on the basis of searching for the material leaven, Paul draws the lesson of the believer removing the insidious leaven of corruption within and upholds the ideal of holiness to the Lord.

IDENTITY

At the close of each Seder is repeated the hope that the next year it may be celebrated in Jerusalem. Even though Israel today is a Jewish state, the formula is still repeated, with a sense of fulfillment and in anticipation of the coming of the Messiah.

FEAST OF UNLEAVENED BREAD

IN ANCIENT TIMES

According to Leviticus 23:6-8, the Passover was separate from the Feast of the Unleavened Bread, which was to be-

gin on the fifteenth day of the month Nisan. The significance of the order of the Passover and Feast of Unleavened
Bread has been lost because it has not been possible to sacrifice the Passover lamb since the destruction of the Temple. The terms are now used interchangeably; originally
they were distinct.

FIRSTFRUITS

This sacrifice was offered on the second day of the Feast
of Unleavened Bread, when a sheaf of the first ripe ears of
the barley harvest was presented. In the time of the second
Temple it involved elaborate preparation and ceremony.

Israel was taught in this ceremony, especially following
the Passover, that not only they themselves but all of their
possessions belonged to the Lord. In presenting the firstfruits, they consecrated the entire harvest, since the blessing of the fruit of the land was tied up with their obedience
to God. The ceremony also involved a pledge of harvest on
God's part.

The material offering, however, was a symbol of the spiritual reality. The New Testament refers to this when it
describes the Messiah as the firstfruits of the redeemed of
God (1 Co 15:23) —of the world's spiritual harvest of Jewish and Gentile believers.

FEAST OF WEEKS

DIFFERENT NAMES

The Feast of Weeks, *Shavuot,* is indicated in Leviticus
23:15-18. It is called the Feast of Harvest (Ex 23:16) of
the wheat grain. It is also designated as the Day of Firstfruits (Num 28:26), besides the Feast of Weeks (Ex 34:22;
Deu 16:10).

It is known as Pentecost, since it was celebrated fifty days
from the second day of Passover and ended the days of the
counting of the 'omer. The feast is observed today in May
or June. Pentecost is also known as the time of the giving

of the Law, since it was believed that Moses received the Law on that day. This could very well be, inasmuch as the children of Israel, after going out from Egypt at Passover time, arrived at Sinai about two months later.

IN THE SYNAGOGUE

The special readings in the synagogue are on the first day, Exodus 19; 20; Ezekiel 1; and on the second day, Deuteronomy 15:19—16:17; Habakkuk 3. The book (*megillah*) of Ruth is also read, because Ruth was a proselyte to Judaism and also because of the book's references to the harvest festival and the treatment of strangers and the poor.

Another reason for the importance of the Law, or *Torah*— and therefore of this feast in the Jewish mind—is that it no doubt was the means of the preservation of the Jewish people after the city of Jerusalem and the Temple were destroyed and the people were dispersed. They then became the people of the Book, and their study and adherence to its laws maintained their identity and distinctiveness.

IN THE HOME

In the home, the feast is characterized chiefly by the eating of honey and milk, which are said to stand for the Law and learning; in turn these are sweet and nourishing. Decorations of greens, flowers, and branches, in both the home and snyagogue, represent the land and harvest (grain). The observance of this ceremony is a good indication that through the Dispersion, wherever and under whatever circumstances the Jewish people lived, they always cherished a hope for a return to their ancient land.

NEW TESTAMENT PARALLELS AND SPIRITUAL EMPHASIS

Out of a number of parallels that could be mentioned, we note that the New Testament presents Messiah Jesus as the firstfruits of the redeemed. It goes even further and speaks of the events that happened at Pentecost as a firstfruits representing the Church. In its turn the Church itself, as a sort of firstfruits taken from among men of all nations and tongues (Acts 15:14), is a pledge of a fuller harvest to be gathered in dispensation of the fullness of the times.

NINTH OF 'AV

EXPLANATION

Of the several minor fasts, the *Ninth of 'Av (Tishah b'Av)* is the most important. It occurs on the ninth day of the Jewish month of 'Av, about two months after Shavuot. This would correspond to sometime during July or August. This is a day set aside to remember several tragic events in Israel's history: the anniversary of the destruction of both Temples and the expulsion of Jewish people from Spain in 1492.

IN THE SYNAGOGUE

In the synagogue, the veil in front of the Holy Ark is replaced by a black drape or the opening to the Holy Ark is left bare. Worshipers remove their shoes and sit on low stools or on the floor. All prayers are said in a low tone of mourning. The reading is from the book of Lamentations.

The Sabbath following the ninth of 'Av is called the Sabbath of comfort, since on that day Isaiah 40 is read as a passage of comfort and hope for the future; even in the book of Lamentations there is a final emphasis on comfort, with the prayer to "renew our days as of old" (Lam 4:21, KJV).

IN THE HOME

In the home, the meal before the fast includes eggs (often a symbol of mourning) and also a pinch of ashes. This is a picture of grief too strong for words.

IN ISRAEL

Israelis in the land visit the Western Wall (formerly referred to as the Wailing Wall) on that day to mourn and weep in prayer. It is customary to encircle the walls of Old Jerusalem in procession ending at the Western Wall.

NEW YEAR

GENERAL

Rosh Hashanah marks the beginning of the Jewish civil New Year, and the name means "beginning of the year." It occurs on the first day of the seventh month on the religious calendar, the month Tishri, corresponding to the September-October period. The civil and spiritual are seen as inseparably united in these festivals.

On the Saturday evening before Rosh Hashanah, *Selihot* begins. These are special prayers of repentance and forgiveness, uttered every night during this period. The word comes from the Hebrew root *salah,* which means "to forgive."

Rosh Hashanah is not the biblical name for this festival, since this name occurs only once (Eze 40:1). It is more properly called "Memorial of Blowing" (Lev 23:24), "Day of Blowing" (Num 29:1), or "Day of Judgment," although today's popular name is Rosh Hashanah. The *shofar*[6] has a solemn significance in Scripture (Amos 3:6; Ex 19:16; Eze 33:3). Blowing the shofar was a call to gather for worship or warfare, as well as a call to judgment and repentance. In connection with this festival, the number seven is also of particular significance. Every new moon (*rosh hodesh*)[7] was a solemn occasion, but this was the seventh new moon and therefore most solemn.

In the Bible, the Memorial of Blowing was to bring to mind something present or to come. The Feast of Trumpets was to remind Israel of its need of repentance in prepa-

6. The Hebrew term for the horn of a ram. It had a varied use, but on this occasion it was sounded a number of times during these holy days. The blowing of the shofar is called *teru'ah* (blowing).
7. The words *rosh hodesh* actually mean the new month ("beginning of the month") since Israel has a lunar calendar, the new moon and the new month coincide.

ration for the Day of Atonement, which soon followed. Also, in the "blowing," a note of joy was expressed, since it announced pardon on the basis of the sacrificial offering.

In the Home

In the home, after evening service in the synagogue, there is little to distinguish this festival from the Sabbath. The candles are lit in the same manner as on the Sabbath.

It is the common custom to dip bread or an apple in honey to symbolize the hope of sweetness in the year to come. The festival is a time of greeting, the common expression being *Shanah tovah*, "A good year." Sometimes the longer expression is used: *Leshanah tovah tikkatev*, or, "May you be inscribed for a good year" (to be inscribed implies being recorded in the book of life).

In the Synagogue

Many special prayers are said in the synagogue on this festival, addressing God particularly as Judge and King. The climax of the service is the blowing of the shofar, beginning with the recitation of Psalm 37 seven times. Two days are observed among Traditional Jews in order to be sure that the right day is celebrated. This has its origin in ancient times, when there was uncertainty involved in transmitting the signal to commence the festival (a new moon) to remote places.

Tashliḥ

This interesting ceremony of *tashliḥ* is still observed by Traditional Jews on the afternoon of the first day. It consists of throwing bread crumbs, sometimes emptying the pockets, into a body of water, repeating at the same time Micah 7:18-20, especially the phrase, "Thou wilt cast all their sins into the depths of the sea" (v. 19). The word *tashliḥ* is the Hebrew for "thou wilt cast."

THE TEN DAYS

The ten days between Rosh Hashanah and Yom Kippur are called the Ten Days of Repentance. At the end of these days people say to one another, "May the final verdict be favorable." These days are also called the terrible, or dreadful, days because of the great solemnity and uncertainty of judgment.

REPENTANCE

Among the Orthodox a few of the devout men wear their burial shroud as an incentive to sincere repentance, because it reminds them of mortality, uncertainty of life, and divine judgment. Throughout these days there is also confession of guilt and petition for forgiveness one to another.

DAY OF ATONEMENT

GENERAL

During the second century B.C.E., the Day of Atonement, Yom Kippur, was already called the "Great Day," or "The Day." Jews of other lands turned their eyes toward the Temple at that time. During the Temple period, the high priest himself performed the ceremony in the Temple; on the other days he only showed himself.

Yom Kippur is the only fast ordained in the Scriptures (Lev 16:1-34; 23:27-32; Num 29:7-11). There were other feasts, but this was the only one appointed by law. The great purpose of this day (Lev 16:33) was to make atonement for the holy sanctuary, the tabernacle of the congregation, the altar, the priests, and all the people. It was a time of national confession and of personal atonement for sins not confessed and forgiven during the year.

The observance of this day has a strong undergirding in the Scriptures, and tradition has built upon this. Yom Kippur, also called the Day of Judgment, is the culmination of the ten days of repentance. The Day of Atone-

ment is regarded by Jewish people as the day of the account-
ing of the soul. They picture God as putting on the robes of
a judge and weighing the good deeds of each person on one
side of a balance against the evil deeds on the other side.
The verdict depends upon which way the scale tips. Consequently, Jewish people perform many good deeds during
the ten days preceding this day, with much prayer and repenting, in the hope that the scale will be tipped on the
right side and the sins forgiven.

KOL NIDRE

The evening service in the synagogue begins with the
Kol Nidre, a canted prayer. The rabbis and sages disagreed
as to the use of the Kol Nidre on this occasion, but in time
this appealing and strange melody and prayer did become
associated with Yom Kippur. The words *Kol Nidre* mean
"all vows"; the prayer is an appeal to God for release from
vows made during the year. Its origin is said to have been
in the Middle Ages, when Jewish people were often forced
to take vows under compulsion, particularly regarding baptism into the so-called Christian faith. This was an appeal
to God to be released from these vows. For this reason the
enemies of the Jews would say that the word of a Jew was
worthless, because on Yom Kippur such a word could be
made null and void. The Jewish people, in reply, have in-
sisted that a word given against one's own conscience is not
valid.

PRAYERS IN THE SYNAGOGUE

A number of scripture passages are specified for Yom
Kippur, and during the day many interesting prayers are
uttered. The high point in a traditional synagogue service
is the utterance of the word *prostration,* when all in the congregation throw themselves to the floor and bury their faces
in confession. Some devout Jewish men stay in the synagogue for the entire twenty-four hours, weeping and con-

fessing sins (although the younger generation today hardly does this).

MEMORIAL

A memorial is held for souls of relatives and friends and those who have suffered death from persecution. Those whose parents are still alive leave the synagogue at this time, because many children bear the names of their grandparents and these names would be mentioned in the prayers. It is considered an ill omen or just bad taste to have present those who have the same names as the departed.

CLOSING EMPHASIS

The closing prayer service of the day is called $n^{e'}ilah$ ("shoe," "sandal"). It is called by this name because it was recited at the time when the shoes were put on, preparatory to going home. It referred originally to the closing of the Temple gates and was interpreted later to mean the closing of the gates of heaven. It represents a final opportunity for penitence with the whole heart and for pleading for a good year. The service closes with one long blast of the shofar. Following this, there is a great shout of response from the congregation, "Next year in Jerusalem!" although for the Traditional in Israel today there is the anticipation of Messiah's soon coming.

SPIRITUAL SIGNIFICANCE

Yom Kippur was Israel's day of reconciliation and has prophetic significance as it points to the future day of national repentance when the iniquity of the land will be removed in a day (Zech 3:9; 7:9—13:9).

Every fiftieth year on the Day of Atonement, the complete cycle of seven sevens of years was fulfilled, and the Jubilee proclaimed liberty for people and land (Lev 25:9-10). This is also a forecast of the time when the Messiah will give liberty to the captives of Israel, and the earth itself will enjoy its rest.

FEAST OF THE TABERNACLES

The Feast of Tabernacles (*Ḥag Hasukkot*) was a most important festival in Bible times and is designated in both the Bible and the Talmud as "the Festival of the Lord." It was a thanksgiving week in Israel and marked the end of the grain harvest, the final ingathering. It was also one of the three pilgrimage festivals and started five days after Yom Kippur.

Other names for this feast are the Feast of Booths (Lev 23:34; Neh 8:15-16) and the Feast of the Ingathering; it is also referred to as "the season of our rejoicing." In ancient times Temple ceremonies included joyful processions with the waving of branches (the *lulav* [palm branch], myrtle, willow branch, and *'etrog* [citron]) and the singing of the *Hallel* psalms (Ps 113-118). The procession went around the altar once each day in the Temple and seven times on the seventh day.

PURPOSE

The purpose of Sukkot was to remind the Israelites that they lived in the wilderness only temporarily, until they reached the settled abode of the promised land. For this reason the *sukkah* ("booth"), was a flimsy structure. It still serves to remind Israel, after two thousand years of wandering and uncertainties, that they have no permanent home or land and that they frequently have been an unwelcome and unwanted people.

OBSERVANCE

For this festival Traditional and Conservative Jews build a sukkah in the yard or on their roof. It is loosely covered with branches so that it admits both rain and sun and so that the sun may be seen by day and the stars by night. Here the devout spend as much time as possible both in prayer and at meals, considering the past and hoping for the future. It is loosely constructed to remind the people that life is temporary. Sides and walls are decorated with fruits and flowers. Among the Reform Jews, it is customary to have a communal sukkah at the temple with a prescribed service.

Four species of branches are used in the celebration, the lulav (palm branch), myrtle, willow, and 'etrog (citron). In the synagogue during services and in the sukkah each day, the branches are shaken together during appropriate passages or blessings in the service. The lulav is held in the right hand. The myrtle with three twigs and the willow with two are attached to it. The 'etrog is held in the left hand. These are brought into the sukkah at home every morning. Each member of the family holds them and shakes them in the prescribed manner while pronouncing a blessing. They are also carried in the daily procession in the synagogue. These represent the general harvest.

SYNAGOGUES

The morning services have several features. There is the chanting of the Hallel, Psalms 113-118, with lulav and 'etrog in hand, symbols of harvest and thanksgiving. There is also a procession led by the cantor, followed by the rabbi and those of the congregation who possess lulav and 'etrog. The ark is opened, and the procession marches down the aisle, singing Psalm 118. On the first two days, the scripture passages read are Leviticus 22:26—23:44; Numbers 29: 12-16; and Zechariah 14:1-21. There are also other prescribed passages.

GREAT DAY OF THE FEAST

The great day of the feast is the seventh day of Sukkot and is considered its most solemn day. There is an ancient tradition that the season of judgment really ends on this day rather than on Yom Kippur. Some wear their shrouds as on Yom Kippur. The procession with lulav and 'etrog is repeated seven times on this day in the synagogue. Many also beat willow branches on the ground. (This is the great day of the feast mentioned in John 7:37.)

CROWNING FEAST OF ALL FEASTS

The crowning feast of all feasts is the eighth day of Solemn Assembly, although according to Leviticus 23:36 it may be thought to be a separate festival. The eighth day has spiritual significance. As one has indicated, the Feast of Booths is the only biblical festival that has an octave, concluding with "the last and great day of the feast." This can be the conclusion or crowning feasts of all feasts of the year. This is the day Israelites returned to their homes to rejoice there and to begin a new cycle. The New Testament seems to catch the significance here and points to the final rest of all God's creatures (Rev 21:1-8), where "the tabernacle of God is with men, and he will dwell with them, and they shall be his people" (v. 3, KJV).

GLADNESS OF THE LAW

Simḥat Torah, the Rejoicing of the Law, is really a ninth day of the great festival of Sukkot. On this day the reading of the Law is completed in the synagogue and begins anew with Genesis 1. This is done to avoid any break in the liturgical reading.

The eve of this festival presents a very joyful scene in the synagogue. In a special procession, the *hakkafot,* all the scrolls of the Law are taken out of the ark and carried around till everyone has carried one of the scrolls. All kiss the scrolls and sing and dance in honor of the Law. In this way there is an expression of the great love for the Torah. (It must be remembered that a younger generation of Jewish people in America knows little about the Word of God.)

SPIRITUAL SIGNIFICANCE

The Feast of Sukkot finds its fullness in a Messianic age, as made plain in Zechariah 14. As already indicated, it naturally follows Israel's great day of national repentance and confession (Zech 12:10-14), cleansing (Zech 13:1), and restoration to God in a final ingathering. But Sukkot has also universal fulfillment in a future harvest and ingathering of nations to God, and the festival will be observed as a memorial after that (Zech 14:16). Even in ancient Jewish writings this festival was regarded as prophetic as well as commemorative.

ḤANUKKAH

HISTORICAL BACKGROUND

Ḥanukkah means "dedication" and refers to the dedication of the Temple in the year 164 B.C.E. after it was cleansed from the desecration by the Syrian king Antiochus Epiphanes. Ḥanukkah is not mentioned in Hebrew Scriptures, since the canon was closed around 420 B.C.E. The story is found in the books of the Maccabees in the Apocrypha, and there is mention of it in the gospel of John 10: 22-23. Ḥanukkah commemorates a great and decisive victory over the Syrian king, preserving not only the land and the liberty of the Jewish people but, of far more significance, their religion and worship and the knowledge of the one true God.

After the death of Alexander the Great, the Grecian empire was divided into four parts among four of his generals. One of the kingdoms was Egypt, ruled by the group called the Ptolemies; and another was Syria, ruled by the Seleucids. The land of Israel lay between these two kingdoms and was ruled first by one and then by the other. The Hellenism of Alexander was perpetuated by Syria and Egypt, and when Syria came to dominate the land of Israel in 198 B.C.E., the Hellenistic culture was forced on the people.

Efforts to hellenize the Jews were intensified by Antiochus Epiphanes when he came to power in 175 B.C.E.

The period in history was one of political turmoil. Antiochus attempted to conquer Egypt but failed, and on the way back to Syria from Egypt he proceeded to Jerusalem. There he desecrated the Temple by offering a pig on the altar and sprinkling its broth over the holy vessels. He forbade the practice of the Jewish religion—particularly observance of the Sabbath, reading and study of the Law, and the rite of circumcision. He also ordered the Jews to erect altars everywhere, to offer abominations on them, and to worship Greek gods. He introduced the Greek games, which were foreign and repulsive to the Jewish spirit and religion.

Led by a devout and heroic old priest, Mattathias, and his five sons, the most noted of whom was Judas, the Jewish people revolted against the Syrians. After several years of guerrilla warfare, the Jewish armies, displaying great heroism and aided by providential circumstances, decisively defeated the large Syrian armies. Jerusalem was recaptured, and the Temple was cleaned and dedicated.

It was highly providential that the Jews were able to successfully repel the inroads of the Hellenistic culture and idolatry. Apart from scattered colonies of Jews in the Dispersion, the land of Israel was the only place on earth where the one true God was worshiped and His name known. At a cost of many lives and great suffering, the Jewish people preserved the Scriptures and the knowledge of God. They kept the way clear for the Messiah's appearance and the great redemption to come, according to Scripture.

OBSERVANCE

Home. Ḥanukkah begins on the twenty-fifth day of *Kislev,* which corresponds to the period of November-December. On this day the Temple was rededicated. The observance lasts for eight days and is regarded as a minor festival. There is no particular custom of worship in the synagogue and there is no necessity to abstain from work. It is celebrated joyfully, not only as a reminder of a great past deliverance but also as a symbol of hope for the future.

It is particularly celebrated by the kindling of lights. A special candlestick (ḥanukkiah) containing eight lights is used.[8] The usual method is to light one candle on the first evening, two candles on the second evening, and so on until all eight are kindled on the last night.

The festival is celebrated for eight days because of a miracle said to have taken place at the time of the rededication of the Temple, after Judah won religious freedom from the Seleucids. There was only enough oil to fuel the perpetual light in the Temple for one day. But the day's supply of oil is said to have lasted miraculously for the eight days until proper additional oil was found.

Ancient times. Hanukkah was celebrated in ancient times with a great illumination of the Temple accompanied by the singing of the Hallel, Psalms 113-118, while people carried palm branches. Private homes also were illumined. Second Maccabees 10:6 indicates that all this was after the manner of the celebration of the Feast of Tabernacles.

Modern times. The festival is celebrated today with particular zest and joy in Israel, the scene of the ancient victories and deliverance, upon the very soil which received the blood of its heroes and martyrs. The celebration is especially meaningful in Israel as Israelis fight to maintain their position in the land. Hanukkah is a symbol of living in a free, independent land.

The lights of the ḥanukkiah are kindled in the synagogue and in the home, accompanied by the recitation of special benedictions.

8. The ḥanukkiah, a candlestick of eight lights used only for Hanukkah, is not to be confused with the menorah of seven branches which stood in the Holy Place of the Temple.

PURIM

HISTORICAL BACKGROUND

The Feast of *Purim* has its origin in the time of Esther, when Ahasuerus was king of Persia (484-464 B.C.E.). The name was taken from the word *pur* ("lot") because Haman cast a lot to determine the day when Jewish people throughout the Persian empire would be destroyed. The name therefore is Feast of Lots.

OBSERVANCE

The Feast of Purim is celebrated on the fourteenth day of the month Adar, the twelfth month of the Jewish calendar, or in the second month Adar when it is leap year. This would correspond to our period of February-March. The feast is celebrated in synagogue, home, and wherever possible in the community. It is a day of joy and fun rather than a holy day.

In the synagogue, the book of Esther is read, not from an ordinary text of the Hebrew Scriptures but from a parchment scroll called *megillah* ("rolled up"). When the name *Haman* is read, there is generally a stamping of feet, clapping of hands, and shaking of rattles, especially among the young—even in the synagogue. Women attend particularly because of the important part played by Esther.

On this day the people give gifts to family and friends, and also give to the poor. It is now often the occasion of family reunions. In the home, a special delicacy called *haman-tashen,* a three-cornered cooky made of dough filled with poppy seeds, is eaten.

Purim is characterized in Israel today by masquerades, plays, and pantomimes of all kinds. The story of Esther has always been a source of comfort and hope to Jewish people; in the darkest hours of affliction and distress, God will send them deliverance. It is a remarkable book of the providence of God, even though the name of God is not once mentioned in it.

FOR FURTHER STUDY

BOOKS

Buksbazen, V. *The Gospel in the Feasts of Israel.* Philadelphia: Friends of Israel, 1954. This is a presentation of the holidays by a Messianic Jew.

Epstein, I. *Judaism.* Baltimore: Penguin, 1959. This study from the Jewish point of view is by the editor of the Soncino edition of the Babylonian Talmud.

Gaster, T. *Festivals of the Jewish Year.* New York: Sloan, 1953. Gaster, a prolific Jewish writer, presents a more critical view of the scriptural assertions.

Heller, A. M. *The Vocabulary of Jewish Life.* New York: Hebrew Publ., 1942. Many of the terms of Judaism come up in the areas of holidays and customs.

Kligerman, A. J. *Feasts and Fasts of Israel.* Baltimore: Emmanuel Neighborhood House, 1931. Kligerman is an outstanding Messianic Jewish figure of a past generation.

Lehrman, S. M. *The Jewish Festivals.* London: Shapiro, Vallentine, 1953.

Rosenau, W. *Jewish Ceremonial Institutions and Customs.* New York: Bloch, 1939.

Schauss, H. *Guide to Jewish Holy Days.* New York: Schocken, 1969. This volume and the previous two are written from the Jewish point of view.

FILMSTRIPS

Judaism. Life Filmstrips. New York: Time-Life. This is part of a series on comparative religions, distributed by LIFE Education Program, Box 834, Radio City P.O., New York, N.Y. 10019.

The Jewish Home. New York: Jewish Ed. Com. of N.Y.

4

JEWISH CUSTOMS AND PRACTICES

INTRODUCTION

There are many customs and practices in the Jewish religion, but we do not have the space in this brief chapter to treat them all in depth. Some of the more important ones will be mentioned so that the Christian will have a basic knowledge of the customs.

THE SYNAGOGUE

As far as we know, the synagogue originated during the intertestamental period, although there were traces of it even earlier, during the Exile in Babylon. Insofar as the Jewish religious practice in America has decreased, synagogue attendance also is in decline. However, until the world wars, the synagogues in the old Jewish communities were the center of Jewish life. I urge you to attend some Jewish services at the synagogue and Reform Jewish temple to become acquainted with the order of service and with the articles of furniture and decoration inside the place of worship.[1]

ORDER OF SERVICE

No matter what kind of place of worship it is—Orthodox synagogue, Conservative synagogue, or Reform temple—its central point of interest is always the pulpit area.

1. Many rabbis will welcome Christian groups in the services, conduct tours of the synagogue or temple, and explain the procedure and arrangement in their place of worship. It is best to call ahead so that the rabbi can make the necessary preparations.

At the pulpit the rabbi reads the service and delivers the sermon. Sometimes there is a second pulpit where the cantor chants the prayers. Sometimes there are two small pedestals: one holding candles lit in observance of the beginning of the Sabbath or a holiday, and the other holding the *kiddush* (sanctification) cup of wine, over which prayers of thanksgiving are offered for the blessings that people have experienced.

Reform Jewish temples and many Conservative synagogues use a choir and organ to accompany the rich liturgy of Judaism. In some places the choir can be heard and seen, while in other places the choir is only heard. In some of these congregations there is also the cantor (*ḥazzan*), who sings and directs the music. In orthodox synagogues, the beautiful hymns and melodies are sung without musical accompaniment.

ARRANGEMENT

The holy ark, *'aron kodesh,* is the central shrine of every Jewish house of worship. The finely built cabinet stands at the front of the sanctuary. In it the Torah in scroll form with appropriate portions from the prophets interspersed is placed. In some congregations a beautifully decorated mantle hangs in front of the ark doors. Other congregations merely emphasize the beauty of the doors themselves. A phrase frequently appears above the ark doors: "Know before whom you stand."

On each side of the ark is a seven-branched candelabra, the *menorah.* On the wall above the ark are placed the tablets of the Ten Commandments. These are inscribed in Hebrew and usually contain the first two words of each commandment. Hebrew is written from right to left, and therefore the first commandment is on the upper right as one faces the tablet. Often a lion is on each side of the tablets, and above the tablet is a crown. This emphasizes the enthronement of the Word and its importance to the people. The sovereignty of the Torah and learning are watchwords in the life of the faithful.

In front of the commandments is the eternal light, the *ner tamid,* which burns at all times. It reminds us that God and the Jewish way of life are not just temporal but also have eternal consequences.

Inside the holy ark there is the Torah. Since the Torah is very sacred to the Jewish people, congregations often have several. The scrolls may vary in size, but each has the same contents: the five books of Moses. A portion of the Torah is assigned to each week of the year so that the entire scroll is read every year. *Simḥat torah* is the time when the lectionary cycle finishes with the book of Deuteronomy and begins again with the book of Genesis.[2]

The Torah is written in Hebrew, with special ink on parchment. A scribe writes the Torah in a special, prescribed manner; he must not make any mistake. If he does, he cannot erase but must rewrite the entire section.[3]

The ornaments in which the Torah is wrapped have an extremely interesting story. Their origin can be traced to the vestments and ornaments of the high priest, who served in the Temple in Jerusalem. After the Temple was destroyed, the garment symbols of the high priest were transferred to the Torah. The crown on the head of the high priest became the crown placed on top of the rollers upon which the parchment is rolled; this crown is now the "crown of learning." The bells which the high priest used as ornaments are now placed on the ends of the rollers. The flowing white robe of the high priest is now the mantle (covering) of the *Torah.* The breastplate which was worn

2. The cycle reading never finishes with the book of Deuteronomy, but the last reading includes the last of Deuteronomy and the first part of Genesis, thus emphasizing that the reading of the Word is never to be finished. See "Gladness of the Law" in chap. 3.
3. For further information concerning all the rules in copying the Scriptures, see the Tractate *Sopherim* in the Babylonian Talmud.

by the high priest as he ever bore the names of the tribes of the nation upon him is now placed on the Torah covering and hung by a silver chain from the roller edges. Many times the Torah covering itself is decorated with symbols—for example, the crown, the breastplate, or the lions of the tribe of Judah. To aid the person reading from the Torah, a pointer is provided. At the end of it is a pointing finger; this is called *yad,* which in this case means "finger." No one who reads the Torah ever puts his own finger on the parchment itself.

Jewish prayer books are used in the service. Some are written only in Hebrew, but others have both Hebrew and English. The regular prayer book is called *siddur.* For the services of Rosh Hashanah and Yom Kippur, a special prayer book is used.

WORSHIP

The men of Conservative and Traditional congregations follow the custom of wearing a head covering during prayer. A skull cap (yiddish, *yarmulke;* or Hebrew, *kepah*) is usually available at the entrance to the synagogue. Women usually wear hats. In the Reform temple, men do not cover their heads in worship. In the Orthodox synagogues and in the more strict Conservative synagogues, the women sit separated from the men. Sometimes a balcony is reserved for the women. In Reform temples the men and women can sit together.

Conservative and Traditional men wear a prayer shawl called a *tallit* during some of the services. They also wear the phylacteries, or *tefillin,* during morning services, except those on the Sabbath and holidays. Phylacteries are small, cubical boxes which contain passages of Scripture. The boxes are bound to the left arm and the forehead by means of leather straps. Reform Jews do not wear the tallit or tefillin during the services.

THE HOME

A practicng Jewish household is the scene of many religious rites and celebrations and is hallowed by spiritual significance and sacred ministry. Particularly in the days of the Dispersion and in times of persecution it was a little sanctuary.

MEZUZAH

The first object noticed on entering the home is the *mezuzah.* Fastened to the right doorpost is a long, narrow case of metal or wood containing a parchment on which is inscribed Deuteronomy 6:4-9 and 11:13-20. Devout Jews touch their fingers to the mezuzah and then to their lips as in a kiss, on entering or leaving a room, as an act of endearment for the Scriptures it contains. It has become the symbol of a Jewish home, a sign of acceptance of God's Law and of God's presence within, and a reminder of the need for purity and the sanctity of life.

KASHRUT

The dietary laws (*kashrut*) are based on the permissions and prohibitions regarding the foods one can eat, described in the Bible (Lev 11). However, the Scripture has been amplified by tradition, which goes far beyond biblical injunction. The word *kasher* means "clean," or "fit to eat." It has been one of the most important factors in the preservation of Jewry as a distinct people, since it prevented them from mingling freely with others, particularly at meals. The forbidden foods are mainly meats and fish.

SHᵉḤITAH

Even animals which may be eaten must be slaughtered in a special way. This is usually performed by a special Jewish slaughterer called a *shoḥet.* The knife used is of prescribed measurements and keenness to render the slaughter-

ing as humane as possible and to insure the quickest drain-
ing of blood. In Hebrew thinking, blood and life are syn-
onymous (Lev 17:11) ; therefore, no blood is eaten at all.
The blood is sacred and highly respected. In addition to
this, meat is soaked in water for half an hour, kept in salt
for a full hour, and then rinsed. Only after this procedure
is it ready for preparation.

The more traditional of the Jewish people have two sets
of kitchen utensils and tableware—one for dairy products
and one for meat. Milk foods of any kind must not be eaten
soon after meat foods. The rabbis base this practice of not
mixing milk and meat on the verse, "You are not to boil a
kid in the milk of its mother" (Ex 23:19). However, in
this passage Moses was forbidding the Israelites to adopt the
Canaanite's pagan rite for insuring fruitful crops. They
took a kid, or other newborn animal, and made a broth of
the cooked meat of the kid and the milk of its mother; then
the broth was poured out on the fields. Therefore, there is
no valid basis for this traditional injunction of separating
milk and meat.

Brit Me'ilah

Brit me'ilah, the "covenant of circumcision," is performed in the home when the male infant is eight days old.
This observance is so important that it may be performed
even on the Sabbath. It is an elaborate ceremony attended
by many relatives and friends. Circumcision is performed
by a *mo'el,* one specially trained for the operation. The
person holding the child is the godfather, *sandek.* The child
is placed on a special chair called Elijah's chair. All stand
during the ceremony, and a joyful feast follows it. Today
the circumcision is usually performed by a doctor at the
hospital, and then the feast is celebrated on the eighth day
in the home. This extremely important observance in Jewish life has served to maintain the separateness of the Jewish people.

PIDYON HABEN

Pidyon haben means the "redemption of the son"; the ceremony is called also the "redemption of the firstborn" (*pidyon hab^ehor*). A male child who is a firstborn must be redeemed after the age of thirty days (Ex 13:13). At this festive ceremony, performed in the home, appropriate prayers are said and a certain sum specified as redemption money is given to a *cohen* ("priest"), or descendant of Aaron.[4] This practice is not followed very much anymore.

BAR MIṢVAH

The term *bar miṣvah* means "son of the commandment." The bar miṣvah ceremony is observed on the thirteenth birthday of the Jewish boy. He is now to assume responsibility for keeping the Law, and his father is released from that responsibility for his son. The father praises God for this completion in a prayer during the ceremony. Part of this ceremony is performed in the synagogue, where the boy is called to the lectern with his father to read a portion of the Law on the Sabbath after the boy's birthday. Part of it is celebrated with a feast in the home. It is an occasion of much rejoicing.

The Reform Jew and some Conservatives have a confirmation service for Jewish girls that corresponds to the bar miṣvah; the girl becomes a *bat miṣvah* ("daughter of the commandment"). For the Reform Jew, the occasion for both boys and girls usually takes place on *Shavuot* (Pentecost).

MARRIAGE

Marriage has always been a most sacred ceremony attended with much symbolism. The bride and groom were once expected to fast on the day of marriage as a mark of

---

4. Certain men, either by name or by lineage, are recognized as priests— for example, those who have surnames derived from the names Levi or Cohen. Since there are no records, this is difficult to prove.

penitence for any wrongs committed, although this is hardly practiced today.

At the ceremony Scriptures and prayers are said, and the bride and groom sip from a cup of wine. After the reading of the marriage contract, they partake of another glass of wine. The glass is then broken under heel by the groom, and the priestly benediction is uttered. The breaking of the glass is said to recall the destruction of the Jewish state and Temple because of sin, and the rejoicing of the day is thus tempered by this sad fact. The broken glass is also said to symbolize the frailty of human character; therefore, it incites patience, kindness, and forbearance in the new relationship. It also reminds us of the transitoriness of life.

The most picturesque feature of the ceremony is the *ḥuppah* (canopy) under which the ceremony takes place. It was once the litter in which the bride was carried to the ceremony. Now it stands for the future home and family. It is made of beautiful materials as befits such a symbol.

SHIV'AH

Shiv'ah is the custom of mourning the death of a loved one for seven days in the home. The mourners usually sit on low stools during this period; and visitors do not have to say anything, since their presence is a symbol of grief mutually shared. On return from the funeral, there is sometimes a symbolic partaking of a hard-boiled egg, as well as having ashes present: all are symbols of mourning.

THE SABBATH

The Sabbath, *Shabbat,* was rather loosely kept in early times, in contrast to the multitude of traditions which hedged it about in later times. The more strict observance began during the Babylonian Exile. This was due to the fact that the Exile was the result of neglect and contempt for the Sabbath. In the Exile, the Sabbath worship began to replace partially the pilgrimage festivals and Temple services and sacrifices. In addition, it also served to distinguish the Jews from non-Jews.

During the time of the second Temple, strictness exceeding the biblical requirements developed. This period also saw the rise of the synagogue and the various religious parties. The synagogue became the center of community life.

In spite of its restrictions and burdensomeness, the Sabbath also was one of the influences which preserved Jewish life throughout Jewry's long night of the Middle Ages. It was an oasis of rest and joy in the midst of dreary and dangerous existence. Synagogue attendance was an event always remembered and awaited with keen anticipation, and Shabbat was a stabilizing influence.

In the Home

In the home, the Sabbath candles are lit seventeen minutes before sundown, and Jewish calendars have the information available so this can be done. The woman of the house repeats appropriate prayers and blessings as she lights the candles. This is the woman's part in the spirituality of Shabbat. She is the queen and can lend her influence to home and family.

On returning from the synagogue, the father recites Proverbs 31:10-31 in praise of the mother, and the males sing *"Shalom Aleicham"* ("Peace Be unto You").

When the family is seated at the table for the evening meal, the ceremony of *kiddush* is performed. A glass of wine is taken, over which a special blessing is said. After the kiddush everyone tastes the wine as a symbol of good cheer and a reminder of the two reasons for observing Shabbat: the creation of the world and the liberation from slavery in Egypt.

Two loaves of bread called *ḥallot* are on the table. This is bread which is twisted or braided. The two loaves are a symbol of God's bounty as well as a reminder of the double portion of manna on the day before the Sabbath (Ex 16:

22-23). One loaf is cut, then each person at the table receives a small piece. This could remind us of the shewbread in the Temple, representing the sustenance of life. During the meal and after, there are appropriate songs and prayers and also the reading of the Pentateuch passage for the week.

A ceremony called the *havdalah* marks the close of the Sabbath to divide the sacred from the profane. It is performed by inhaling the fragrance of spices in one of a variety of spice boxes—a reminder of the fragrance of life. Wine and milk are also drunk at this time. Then there are Sabbath prayers to ask blessings upon the week. The Sabbath is closed with a greeting one for another, often accompanied by songs about Elijah and Messiah.

SYNAGOGUE

The males of the household go to the synagogue to "welcome the Sabbath," and the special prayer, "Come, My Friend," is chanted. The kiddush ceremony is observed at the close of the Friday evening service. On Saturday morning the Pentateuchal, or Torah, portion (*sedrah*) and an additional portion from the prophets (*haftorah*) are read. It is considered a great honor to be one of the eight persons called to the *bamah* ("platform") to read. Among the Orthodox, many pious Jews spend almost the entire day in the synagogue in the study of the Law or commentaries, although here again this is rarely true among the younger generation today.

It has been said, "More than Israel has kept the Sabbath, the Sabbath has kept Israel" (Aḥad Ha'Am). The Sabbath is the "cornerstone of Judaism." The Sabbath is the vessel that contains the soul of Judaism. As in times past, Sabbath observance was an important factor in the development and preservation of Judaism, so now the lack of observance is an important factor in the decline of the synagogue's usefulness and the waning Jewish identity.

FOR FURTHER STUDY

(See also the list at the end of chap. 3 for information.)

BOOKS

Friedlander, M. *The Jewish Religion.* London: Shapiro, Vallentine, 1953.

Gartenhaus, J. *Unto His Own.* Atlanta: Internat. Brd. of Jewish Missions, 1965. The author of this valuable book is a Messianic Jew.

FILMSTRIPS

Ceremonial Objects of Judaism. Los Angeles: Alexark & Norsim.

5

DOCTRINES OF JUDAISM

SCRIPTURES

What do Jewish people believe about the Scriptures? The Orthodox and the Conservative—particularly the Orthodox—put great emphasis on the validity of Scripture. They have a high regard for the Hebrew Scriptures, the *Tenach*.[1]

Some rabbis teach that the Tenach is inspired in degree; that is, there is a progression in inspiration seen in the various parts of the Hebrew Scriptures. For example, the Ten Commandments are the most important, since they were given in the face-to-face confrontation between God and Moses. The rest of the writings of Moses then follows, and finally the balance of the Hebrew Scriptures stands least in degree of inspiration. Inspiration conceived of in a hierarchy of importance forces us to ask, Is truth wholly or partly true? It would appear that, if all the writers have a God-sanctioned message, then there can be no degrees of importance in the truth of Scripture.

In his thirteen principles of faith, Maimonides devoted principles 6 through 9 to the treatment of the limits of the Word of God. He carefully defined the limits, and in principle 9 he excluded any material that might be added to the canon of the Hebrew Scriptures:

1. As already indicated, it is always best to use the term *Tenach* or *Hebrew Scriptures* when talking with Jewish friends. The term *Old Testament* implies to the Jewish people that it is old and no longer useful because it has been superseded by the New Testament. We do not want to convey this idea to them, so we speak of the *Tenach*.

I believe with perfect faith that this law [the whole law in our possession, principle 8] will not be changed, and that there will never be any other law from the Creator, blessed be His name.

He did not say anything about the New Testament or Koran; he merely indicated that there was nothing more to be added to the Tenach.

Therefore, in faith sharing with our Orthodox or Conservative Jewish friends, there is a basis for discussion as we refer to the Word of God. If the person is agnostic,[2] he will pose problems by raising questions with regard to the validity of the Scriptures. But, when there is a common ground of regard for the Hebrew Scriptures, it is an advantage to share scripture passages.

In chapters 1 and 2 we saw that Reform Judaism originated in Germany, borrowing heavily from a critical biblical scholarship. As a result, Reform Judaism was influenced by higher criticism or the older theological liberalism. In the more recent liberal approach, much of the Tenach is regarded as historical, but this still leaves much to be desired in the concepts of inspiration, authorship, and so forth. The Reform Jew holds that the Scriptures were not inspired in the sense that is understood within conservative theological ranks. The Reform Jew asserts that Moses and Jeremiah and Isaiah were inspired in much the same way that Shakespeare was inspired. An inspired record, to the Reform Jew, is not an inerrant record. Although the Reform, in the later critical approach, may respect items of geography and history, they do assert that men may have made human mistakes in the preparation of the biblical records.

Then how do the Reform Jews use the Scriptures? They use them to stress an ethical base and to derive a moral. I remember speaking with a Reform rabbi who prided him-

2. This term refers to one who neither affirms nor denies the existence of God and other events of the sacred record.

self on the fact that he no longer held the beliefs of his grandfather, who had been an Orthodox rabbi: "I'm not like him anymore." "What do you mean?" I asked. "Well, I don't believe the Scriptures in the way he did." "Well, now, in other words, you *don't believe* that, when Moses came to the Sea of Reeds[3] with the children of Israel, the sea parted and Moses went through with the children of Israel as on dry ground?" He replied, "That is right." I then queried, "What do you do with the event?" He answered, "I just emphasize that God can protect His people." "Rabbi, if you don't believe that the Sea of Reeds did part, then how do you know for sure that God can protect His people?" The point is, if we do not believe the portion of the Word describing the miracle, how can we be sure of the rest?

The Reform Jew's reason for using the Scripture is to find a relevant ethic and moral, but to go beyond this and put credence on the narratives which relate supernatural events is not admitted. The Tenach is recognized as a book of Jewish lore and regarded as a choice body of literature reflecting some of the best efforts of the nation in its developmental period. Today, however, it is not binding except for the lasting principles of ethics and morals.

To be fair, many Reform scholars have now come to recognize the amazing accuracy of the Scriptures in the historical and geographical materials. The archeological work of Nelson Glueck and others has supported the accuracy of the Scriptures by their finds. For some Reform scholars, regard for the authority of the Scriptures has been enhanced, but accounts treating the supernatural are still not received at face value but are rationalized.

---

3. "Sea of Reeds" is the proper translation from Hebrew. This does not detract at all from the miracle which happened, but today we do not know the exact route of the Exodus due to the changes in terrain and of the sea across the centuries.

ORAL LAW

The traditions are an integral part of Judaism. In chapter 1 we considered the development of the traditions during the intertestamental period. These include the Targumim, Mishnah, and Gemara, which were committed to writing by 500 C.E. Since the traditions were not committed to writing until later in Jewish history, they are called "oral Law," in contrast to the written Law. So highly are they valued that many Orthodox consider the basics of the traditions to be on the same level as the written revelation. Furthermore, many Orthodox leaders through the years have held that the main aspects of the traditions were given to Moses by God and existed side by side with the written Word from the inception of Israel as a unified people. There are critical problems in trying to establish an oral Law that dates back to Mount Sinai and Moses, but no one would minimize the veneration of the traditions by the Orthodox and many of the Conservatives.

While the Conservative has a high regard for tradition, he is more amenable to change if conditions warrant it. The "positive historical" principle in Conservative Judaism allows for adaptation in order to continue to practice Judaism in the midst of all the changes of a modern culture. For example, it is considered a very good deed to be in the synagogue on the Sabbath. The traditional Jew has refrained from using any kind of vehicle to go to the synagogue; however, because of modern life's complexities and the distances and time involved in getting to and from the place of worship, the Conservatives ruled that riding in an automobile to the synagogue was not in violation of the tradition. It was felt that the positive values to be gained in synagogue attendance far outweigh the negative effects of riding to the synagogue. So, the Conservative evaluates tradition in light of modern circumstances, while the Orthodox is reluctant to permit any changes (although in America, even the Orthodox have begun to allow some minor changes) .

For the Orthodox and the Conservative, the traditions interpret the Scripture. The written Word is viewed through the traditions. Just as a person wearing sunglasses sees everything colored by the tint of the glass, so the Orthodox and the Conservative see the Word colored by tradition.

The Reform have largely set aside traditions; they keep only a bare minimum of them. The binding authority of tradition is rejected, since the Reform do not view tradition as part of a supernaturally given oral Law. Both written revelation and tradition are considered to have evolved within the growth and development of the Jewish people in the different historical periods. While these writings that distinguish Israel are held in esteem as aids in understanding the background of Judaism, they are not binding to the Reform Jew as an authoritative, inspired record. Therefore, enough tradition may be practiced to provide some kind of Jewish identity, but traditions are dropped freely if they do not fit into the stream of Western culture. (Because of the presence of the state of Israel, many Reform Jews are practicing more of Judaism's traditions.)

GOD

What the Orthodox and the Conservative believe about God is succinctly given in Israel's confession (the *Sh^ema*) : "Hear, O Israel, the LORD our God is one LORD" (Deu 6: 4) . But what is being confessed? The great emphasis is on the one God, the fact that God is one.

This word was given in a day when the rest of the nations worshiped multitudes of idols. The pagan nations had in their pantheons all kinds of gods and goddesses. Some had as many as seven to eight thousand deities as the objects of their devotion. Therefore, Israel's confession was an im-

portant declaration: "We believe in one God!" To this
day, the oneness is emphasized not only by the Orthodox
and the Conservative but by the Reform also.

At this point, however, we should note that many Jewish
people who belong to synagogues or temples and say they
adhere to the Conservative or Reform position will say,
"Yes, we believe in God." But we must probe a bit and
ask, "*What* do you believe about God?" In other words,
we must not take for granted that their belief in God is belief in a personal God. Strange as it may seem, even though
the confession is recited, the Jewish person may very well
not feel that God is a personal Being but that He is some
kind of supreme Power. So it is necessary to probe a bit
further when we discuss their belief in the nature of God.

Whenever some of our Jewish friends respond that they
believe that God is nothing more than a Power or an unde-
finable, impersonal Entity, we need to come back to Deuteronomy 6:4. The confession tells us the kind of God He
is. The implication is that the Lord is a personal God, because He says, "Hear! Listen!" A force does not speak, nor
does some kind of power talk. It takes a distinct personality to speak, to desire to communicate. We can always say to
our Jewish friend—if he is an agnostic or tends to this position—"Look, God is personal. He asks us to listen to
Him."

We could go a step further here to say that He asks us to
listen to Him as He speaks through revelation. The context
of Deuteronomy 6:4 refers to a written communication so
important that it is a guide for every avenue of life. Also,
the word "Hear" is in the imperative mood, emphasizing
that His Word is important. The point is that here is a
personal Being rather than an impersonal force who issues
a command to listen to His written communication.

THE TRINITY

Orthodox, Conservative, and Reform Jews deny the

Trinity,[4] the triune concept of God. They say God is not three; God is one! While a completely satisfactory explanation of the mysterious nature of God has always defied formulation, we can turn to the Scriptures for a clearer understanding of what is meant by "one." One word for "one" is *'ehad,* which can refer to a composite unity, that is, "many which make one." The other word is *yahid,* or "only one." Scripture uses both words.

In Genesis 2:24 we read, "For this cause a man shall leave his father and his mother, and shall cleave to his wife; and they shall become one flesh." The word used here for "one" is *'ehad.* When a man and wife come together and have offspring, then their offspring is one flesh; that is, the one child is the result of a union of two persons, husband and wife. It is referred to as *basar 'ehad,* or "one flesh."

In Numbers 13:17-24, there is the story of the spies who returned from the land of Canaan bringing grapes with them: "Then they came to the valley of Eshcol and from there cut down a branch with a single cluster of grapes" (v. 23). The word for "single" is *'ehad,* a composite unity. It refers to a whole cluster of grapes—"a single cluster" made up of many grapes, not just one grape.

The other word, *yahid,* "only one," is found in Genesis 22:2. God said to Abraham, "Take now your son, your only son," or *"your only one"—yahid.* There is no question here that Abraham had only one son of promise, Isaac. The Spirit of God was very careful when he gave Moses the word *yahid* to describe this situation.

Note again Israel's confession in Deuteronomy 6:4. The word there for "one" in describing the Lord is *'ehad,* or, composite unity—not *yahid.* In other words, there is a compositeness to God's essence or nature. It takes further reve-

---

4. This is a word which does not appear in the Hebrew Scriptures or the New Testament. It was formulated by the Fourth century c.e. from the teachings in the hellenistic branch of the Church of Scripture concerning the mysterious nature of God. Consequently, the term reflects the thinking of that culture; and the usage continues to the present time.

lation to explain what this means. The New Testament speaks of the mystery of God's nature in the terms of the triunity of God. We are not speaking of three gods when we say, "Father, Son, and Holy Spirit"; we are speaking of one God who is a mysterious composite of three Persons. So, when Israel, in the Sh^ema, confesses "one Lord," there is a mystery involved; and in our faith sharing with Jewish friends, we need to point this out. To say that God is only One, ruling out the Persons within this only One by using *yahid* (as Maimonides did in principle 2 of his thirteen principles) is simply asserting something that the Scriptures never said. We need to be scriptural even though we may never completely understand the scriptural concept. We see from the wording of Deuteronomy 6:4 that it was not Moses' intent to avoid a composite description of God. Rather, he was led to express God's nature in this way to allow for the future unfolding of the truth it contains.

Other passages in the Hebrew Scriptures (e.g., Ps 2:79 and Is 48:13-16) hint at this mysterious unity in the nature of God. In Genesis 1:26 we read, "Let Us make man in Our image, according to Our likeness."[5] Here is a reference to a conversation within the triune makeup of God; man in his totality reflects the composite nature of God.

In Proverbs 30:4, a very important passage, note the series of questions that leads to an interesting climax: "Who has ascended into heaven and descended? Who has gathered the wind in His fists? Who has wrapped the waters in His garment? Who has established all the ends of the earth? What is His name—" If we should stop right here and ask our Jewish friend, "Who is the writer talking about?" he would have to honestly say, "He is talking about God."

5. Many rabbis explain this statement by saying that God was talking with the angels and indicating that man would be created in the image of Himself and the angels. Man may have some characteristics of an angel, for example, free will. But this explanation does not fit into the statement by the psalmist in Psalm 8 that man was created to be a little lower than God, certainly a higher position than angels. Genesis 1:26 reflects a conversation between the Persons of the Godhead, and the concepts of image and likeness refer to God Himself.

But we carefully ponder the next question: "Or His son's name? **Surely you know!**" **Many** a Jewish scholar has sought for a solid, satisfactory answer to this question, and the names of different individuals, such as Elijah, have been advanced. But one cannot get away from the import of the question. It is mysterious reference to one of the Persons of the triunity of God.

The Jewish person does not worship idols. He will not worship any kind of image. His confession guards him against this, but at the same time the confession was never meant to preclude a mystery of the Personalities in the one Godhead, which would be further explained in time (though never fully in this life).[6] It is important to be prepared for this issue; because, when we start to share our faith with a Jewish person, this is one of the first things to which he will object: "We don't believe in the Trinity. You Christians worship three gods. We worship one God." We must clarify the biblical concept of God as a triunity, a composite unity.

HOLY SPIRIT

The three groups of Judaism understand *Holy Spirit* to be another term for *God*. They regard God as a Spirit and noncorporeal, that is, He is not to be found in an inanimate object, such as a tree or a stone. He is not limited in any way. Of course, our Jewish friends do not acknowledge the Spirit as One in the triunity of God; the term *Spirit* is recognized as a synonym for God. The function of the Spirit, as seen by the Orthodox and the Conservative, is to encourage men to be godly, inspire men in the preparation of the Scriptures, and help godly men in their pursuit of the study of the Word of God.

6. The Hebrew Scriptures carefully laid down the concept of the one God in the midst of a sea of nations with all their gods and goddesses. Once the concept was securely grasped, the next step was to reveal in the pages of the New Testament something more of the mystery of God's nature. In New Testament times Messiah came to reveal Himself, and the function of the Spirit took on new dimensions.

MAN

The New Testament does not change the Hebrew Scriptures' proclamation that man's nature is sinful; this explains man's inclination toward sin. Because man's nature is sinful, he commits acts of sin and has a potential for evil.

MAN'S NATURE

Orthodox Jews and Conservative Jews deny that man's nature is basically evil and always inclined to do evil. They say instead that a man has a good or evil bent, or inclination.[7] This is a more optimistic view of man. While a man has his evil bent which can tempt him to rebel, he also has his good bent which can respond to encouragement to do good. The reading of the Scriptures, prayer, and doing good deeds enable a man to overcome his evil inclination. Man can conquer evil and achieve good solely through his own free actions; thus, no man is ever bound to sin. If he does yield to temptations, he is solely responsible. Depending on circumstances, temptations, and encouragements, a person can choose to do right or wrong according to whichever bent he is following.

On the other hand, Reform Judaism indicates that man's nature is basically good. All he needs is to be encouraged in order to realize his greatest potential. He encourages this good in himself as he bends his every effort toward the establishment of the kingdom of truth, justice, and peace among all men. In this sense, he cooperates with all men who are interested in the reign of truth and righteousness among men. This basic part of his nature enables a man to pursue the noblest ambitions.

In summary, none of the Jewish theological camps teach

---

7. This is not to be misunderstood as the Christian's two natures, old and new. The Hebrew "bent," or inclination, refers to what a person does when faced with a multitude of choices and influences the moral decisions he makes. Every man is considered to have the capacity to make good moral decisions.

that man is born with a sinful nature which will ultimately condemn him.

Man's Potential

Man's potential is greatly emphasized by the three groups of Judaism, and we agree to some extent with their reasons for this emphasis. Man has the potential to rise to the heights, and he is encouraged to do the best he can. The Orthodox and the Conservative have a well-defined system of ethics to guide man as he seeks to follow his good bent. These encouragements and injunctions appear in the Talmud and other traditional materials as a defined system of works-righteousness to help a person in his endeavors. The Reform Jew encourages a man to fulfill his great potential also; a man can have great hopes and ambitions and perform magnificent services to God and man.

In one sense, we can say that man is a moral being, and he can know what is ethical for society. We all recognize that no man is forced to be a scoundrel. Not *every* man wants to be the inhabitant of skid row or lead a life of alcoholism or dope addiction. He can see injustices and strive with all his might to rectify wrongs and create a better society. Men can be philanthropic with their money and time to service to their fellowman. For example, many Jewish civic leaders are busily engaged in civil-rights movements, striving to better the conditions of men. This is service on the horizontal level, man to man; and it is good in its place. We must admit that a man can do mighty works, even prophesy in God's name and cast out demons (Mt 7:22) ; and most people will realize that this is extremely beneficial for society.

However, we need to ask all our Jewish friends in the various theological camps, "What do the Scriptures say?" We must always come back and recite with our Jewish friends, "Hear, O Israel." What does God want us to hear? He wants us to hear what His Word has to say about man's

nature and potential. God wants us to listen to what the
Hebrew Scriptures say about the barriers that keep a man
from realizing his greatest potential and about the problems
a man has with his nature. And He wants us to see these
plainly described in His Word, not through the screen, or
"sunglasses," of tradition or rationalism or any other of
man's ideas.

THE FALL OF MAN

Concerning man's fall, the Orthodox and Conservative
teach that death is a result of Adam's sin. Adam made the
wrong decision in the Garden of Eden. God had said he
would die if he transgressed the one injunction. This death
is passed on through his descendants. All men die today,
say the Orthodox and the Conservative, as a result of
Adam's actions; but neither of them believes that man's nature has what is known as "original sin." The Jewish view
does not recognize the doctrine that man has an inherited
sinful nature. The Genesis events of man's temptation and
sin are not interpreted as resulting in a condition we know
as the Fall of man. Sin can enter a person's life through re-
bellion, expression of pride, or other failings; but each person commits his own sin. An inherently sinful nature is rejected by the Orthodox and the Conservative. If man has
a sinful nature, this would upset the possibility of man's ful-
filling his potential. Man, as inherently sinful, would be
regarded as being in a prisonhouse and never able to free
himself from the shackles of his sinful nature. This is discussed further in the following sections on sin and salvation, indicating a biblical point of view.

SIN

The Orthodox and the Conservative put a great emphasis
upon sin. The Hebrew language in the Scriptures abounds
with a variety of words that picture sin. Sin is depicted as
an evil bent, crookedness, a twisted morality, and a perver-

sion of righteousness. In comparison with the Greek language, which has about forty words to describe sin, Hebrew has more than a hundred words to describe with fine sensitivity the wide range from varied, bright attractions of sin to the hues of degradation. This extensive depiction is carried over into the traditional materials, which embroider further the multitude of scriptural pictures.

When we read the Talmud and other traditional materials, we can gain a good comprehension of what it means to sin. There are many laws, commandments, and injunctions which spell out correct ethical procedures . If any law is broken, then sin has been committed. As already noted in this chapter, the emphasis of deeds of mercy and righteousness is on the horizontal plane, that is, on man-to-man relationships. Sin is looked upon primarily in this manner. We are not saying that the vertical plane, man-to-God, is not mentioned in the *Talmud* or the traditional writings. It certainly is there: a man can sin against God and will surely reap the consequences. But the great emphasis is on the fact that in sinning, a man harms himself and mistreats his fellowman. Injustices and inequities should be rectified. To harm a fellowman, to cause pain and suffering, or to mar the dignity of man or society is malicious evil.

In Reform teaching, sin is also recognized and depicted, but mainly in its social aspects. The Reform Jew is highly sensitive to the evils of society. The great emphasis of righteousness is upon rectifying the sins of man that have brought about these evils.

SALVATION

From the doctrines of man and sin, we move logically to the Jewish concept of salvation. With our Jewish friends, for the best possible communication, we need to be cautious in the use of the term *salvation*. (We will explore it further under "Atonement," chap. 8.) When a Gentile Christian talks about salvation, he has in mind particular ideas, but Jewish people have other ideas as to its meaning.

In the Hebrew Scriptures, salvation is related to an atonement, a sin offering, a Day of Atonement. While the combination of Scripture and tradition began to develop during the second Temple period, the presence of the Temple and priesthood still made possible a biblical demonstration of salvation. But after the second Temple was destroyed in 70 c.e., and after the subsequent Dispersion of the Jewish people, Jewish scholars substituted for the Temple ritual of the sin offering and the Day of Atonement offerings the "great three concepts," which became in Orthodox and Conservative views the basis for righteousness. These concepts are repentance, *teshuvah;* prayer, *tefillah;* and good deeds, *misvot.*[8] These became the means by which one is made right with God and with his fellow man.

The Jewish view of repentance is turning from sin. A man should turn from his evil deeds, or inclination. He is encouraged to turn toward good bents, and toward doing good things. This is the core idea of repentance: turning from a previous course of action.

There is a great emphasis on the reciting and reading of prayers. Prayer is quite an exercise, especially in an Orthodox synagogue. Those who come for prayer already have on their skull caps, *kipot* (Heb.; or *yarmulkes,* Yiddish), but also put on their phylacteries[9] and their prayer shawls (*talit* with fringes, *sisot*). They take their prayer books and go into a corner or some other spot alone to pray. Everyone

8. After the Temple was destroyed, the substitution of these concepts was introduced as dogma. Even before the Temple was gone, these were already a part of the life of the people; but after the place of sacrifice was destroyed, the three were regarded as equal to sacrifices.
9. The phylacteries are cubes containing portions of Scripture and attached to leather thongs. One cube is placed over the left arm facing the heart, and the thongs are wound around the forearm and hand in a prescribed manner. The other cube is placed on the forehead, and the thongs are placed around the head, with the ends of the thongs hanging down the back. This is in accordance with Deuteronomy 6:8.

prays for himself, loudly or softly, depending on his personality. Prayers are also said by very religious Jews in the home. When they rise in the morning, they go off to some corner to recite and read the morning prayers. The more conservative of Conservative Jewry do likewise. However, only the religious carry on this practice. Most Reform and all secular Jewish folk do not do this at all.

There is also a great emphasis upon good works. The Talmud and traditional writings are filled for the most part with instructions and restrictions concerning good works, misvot. The traditional six hundred and thirteen commandments spell out what every pious Jewish person must do. As already noted, most of these relate to the human relationships of everyday life. It is enjoined that a man do the misvot even if he has problems in other areas of his spiritual life, for example, doubts about God. The concept is that doubts and problems can be resolved as one performs acts of righteousness, since in so doing, a man can be led from thinking merely about himself into thinking of and serving others.

Many people are attracted to Judaism for this reason and because of the high ethical and moral quality of the service of righteousness. A works righteousness is dependent upon the performance of the good deeds as well as prayers and repentance.

Even suffering is an aspect of good deeds. There is a concept in the tradition that, if one suffers, it can be merit on behalf of the needs of others. Other people can borrow a measure of grace or enjoy a merit of mercy from God on the basis of some pious Jewish person's sufferings.

Works righteousness is on the horizontal plane. By this approach the Orthodox and the Conservative hope to establish a righteous relationship with God. In other words, it is the horizontal relationships which, in their thinking, establish the basis for the vertical relationship with God. And yet, even a devout, pious Jewish person, who has been

performing good deeds all his life, will confess that he does
not really know if he personally has a vertical relationship
with God. I have heard this reply all too often.

How is righteousness established, according to the Hebrew Scriptures and New Testament? The picture of the
sin offering in Leviticus 4 indicates the answer very clearly.
When the offerer brought his animal sacrifice, he placed his
hands on the head of the animal and confessed his sins.
The animal then became identified with sins, and this
necessitated the death of the animal, teaching that the pen-
alty of sin is death.

This is only half the picture, however. The action can
be interpreted further as the animal giving its life to the
offerer so that the offerer could continue living. There was
therefore an exchange of life. The animal took the life of
the offerer by identification; and, because the offerer's life
was sinful, the animal died. But the animal gave its life to
the offerer so that he could live. The exchange-of-life principle is the essence of atonement. When an Israelite under
the Mosaic covenant grasped this concept, he experienced
the righteousness of God, or personal salvation. The vertical relationship was established, and the believer could then
go on to realize his greatest potential in a life of service.
God's righteousness would produce a change of heart in the
individual by which he could practice righteousness in his
horizontal relationships to attain the greatest good. In other
words, the Hebrew Scriptures' emphasis was that the vertical responsibility be satisfied *first* in order to have the
right perspective on good deeds. The biblical materials
never spoke of a works righteousness on the horizontal
plane as establishing righteousness with God; it was always
the other way around.

In our faith sharing with our Jewish friends we should
show that the teaching of the Hebrew Scriptures is *not
changed* in the New Testament. The only difference is
that the Messiah now takes the place of the animal. The

exchange-of-life principle remains the same, as seen in 2 Corinthians 5:21: "He [God] made Him [the Messiah] who knew no sin to be sin on our behalf, that we might become the righteousness of God in Him [the Messiah]." The Messiah is now the One who, when we identify with Him, is considered to have died for each of us personally. In return, however, the Messiah gives His life to the believer. The believer receives eternal life, and ultimately he will live in the presence of God. In addition, the life that the believer receives is a life of power that enables him to overcome all barriers and to fulfill his potential. Without the Messiah's quality of life a man can do many good deeds, but these can be tainted by selfish motives, pride, and self-righteousness. There is also the very real problem that, without receiving this victorious life, a person can fall prey to the weaknesses of his own nature, which prevent him from realizing his good aims and goals. In sharing with our Jewish friends we can relate the blessings that God wants to shower upon everyone who will first establish the vertical relationship and will receive the righteousness of God in this exchange of life.

The Jewish view had asserted that man is chained and helpless if he has a sinful nature. While the Jewish point of view wants to see man free to realize his potential, the biblical view is that man is not as free as our Jewish friend thinks he is. Man is forever dogged by a quirk in his nature whereby he continues to fall short of his goals and aspirations (Is 53:6; Ro 3:23). The biblical concept of salvation seen in the exchange-of-life principle is that man may be set free from his quirk, or sin nature, by the dynamic of the life of Messiah. Here is the means of truly realizing one's potential and goals in this life and of the hope of someday being in the presence of God.

As far as the Reform Jew is concerned, salvation is a social matter. The lifelong obligation to do good and to work for the betterment of man and society is for the purpose of saving society. Therefore, salvation to the Reform Jew is largely the remedying of the ills of society in order to establish a more righteous and just world in which to live.

MESSIAH

In our discussion of salvation, we introduced the place of the Messiah in the biblical framework. In faith sharing with our Jewish friends, we use the term *Messiah* for better communication. Our friends will understand, to some extent, that when we say "Messiah," we are talking about Jesus. But, traditionally Jewish people have had a different concept of Messiah; therefore, we must understand each other's usage of the term.[10] We use the term *Messiah* since the word *Christ* can be offensive to our Jewish friends.[11]

The Orthodox and the Conservative believe that the Messiah is an actual person who will come someday to earth; but the Messiah is not regarded as divine. The New Testament asserts that, in some mysterious fashion, Jesus is supernatural as well as human. But the New Testament does not make this assertion in some kind of intellectual vacuum or on the basis of some later interrelation between Gentile Christians and the pagan world. Christians did not borrow the concept of the Son of God from the pagan mystery religions. No, the Jewish New Testament writers testified to the claims of the prophets in the Hebrew Scriptures. For example, Micah 5:2 says that the Messiah is to

10. We should never make the mistake of thinking Jewish people reject the Messiah because they have heard and understood the Gospel message and then knowingly made a decision not to recognize Jesus as the Messiah. Jewish people who believe in a personal Messiah have heard only their own version of the presentation; faith sharing opens up an opportunity for an objective exchange of truths from the Scriptures themselves. Regarding the Person and work of the biblical Messiah, see chap. 7.
11. After studying chapter 2, we can see why Jewish people are apprehensive about hearing of Christ, since so many injustices against them were done by Christendom. But Jewish people were never persecuted in the name of Messiah, and it is the Hebrew term from which the word *Christ* is derived.

be a human governor born in Bethlehem.[12] The passage
goes on to say that His "goings forth [existence] are from
long ago, from the days of eternity," which indicates the
divine origin of the human governor. (See chap. 7 concerning the presentation of the Messiah.)

The Jewish concept of the Messiah considers Him a superhuman inasmuch as he is going to govern the nations in
behalf of God, but He does this as a servant of God while
yet remaining a human being. We need to keep this view
in mind.

This traditional concept was quite well developed by the
first century C.E. Paul declared in 1 Corinthians 15:3, "I
delivered to you as of first importance what I also received,
that Christ died for our sins *according to the Scriptures*"
(italics added). He emphasized, in other words, that the
Messiah died for our sins. This represented a drastic contrast to Paul's training and thinking. He had been schooled
in Jewish thought and tradition that the Messiah was not
divine and that no Messiah was to suffer or die in any way,
especially for sins; rather, he learned, the Messiah was to
come as the great Governor of the nations. So, as Paul drew
from the Hebrew Scriptures, he proclaimed the truth that
the Messiah is divine and that He atoned for our sins
(Mic 5:2; Is 53:6). (Again, see the presentation of Messiah in chap. 8.)

The Reform view holds to an absolute denial of a personal Messiah. Instead, the Reform Jew looks for a golden-
age kingdom that is called Messianic. There is a serious
difference between the Orthodox-Conservative and the Reform ideas of who is to bring in this Kingdom. The former
believe that a personal Messiah will cataclysmically institute the Kingdom. The *Neturai Karta,* an ultraorthodox

12. There is no question that this is a Messianic passage, because when
    Herod asked as to where the Messiah, King of the Jews, was to be
    born, he was told it would be in Bethlehem, and Micah 5:2 was
    quoted. (In the Hebrew Scriptures, the passage is 5:1.)

group in Israel today, will have nothing to do with the government because they feel that, if there is going to be a Messianic age, it is the Messiah who will institute the age; therefore, the present Jewish state and government which is of man is wrong. (Of course, this is an extreme position, and the rest of traditional Jewry in Israel support the present state and the government while also believing in the future ministry of government by the coming Messiah.)

An older Reform Jewish position was that there was no need for the reconstitution of a commonwealth of Israel or the appearance of any personal Messiah before the golden age. By human efforts and good deeds and by their interest in the betterment of society, the Reform hope to institute the golden age. As already stated, the Reform are not exclusive about their efforts; they teach that the cooperation of all good people will create this better world. They therefore rule out the notion of a personal Messiah. However, many Reform Jewish people are reexamining the Scriptures and tradition. While not many will acknowledge the personal Messiah who will establish the Kingdom on earth, there are some second thoughts about denying the centrality of Israel in the scheme of things.

MESSIANIC KINGDOM

The consideration of the Messiah prompts a closer look at the Messianic Kingdom. The Orthodox and the Conservative put a great emphasis upon the future establishment of the Messianic Kingdom—a Kingdom that will be governed by the Messiah on behalf of God. Most feel there will be a day of judgment for the nations at the inception of this Kingdom. There is a conviction that the Messiah will right all wrongs and clear up all national and international problems. Righteousness will then cover the earth as the waters cover the sea. All nations will live in peace. Jerusalem and Israel will be world headquarters for the Messiah in that day, but the Messiah's rule will extend to all nations.[13]

The Reform Jewish people deny a Kingdom presided over by the Messiah. We remember from our first chapter that one of the pioneer Reform leaders, Mendelssohn, said he wanted Jewish people to be German in culture. He meant that Jewish people should come out of the ghettos (of the 1800s) and enter into the Western cultural stream. But for what purpose? Jewish people were to come out of seclusion, enter into Western Gentile life, and make this the means of effecting the golden age. He believed that a growing body of knowledge could be used to eradicate man's injustices and provide for a better society.

Therefore, the Reform emphasize the efforts of men to bring in the Kingdom and are more interested in fitting into current culture than in taking part in the culture and beliefs of their religious counterparts. In denying that the Messianic Kingdom will be instituted in the land of Israel by a personal Messiah, they reject God's promise that He, through the Jewish people reestablished in their own land and under the kingship of their Messiah, will establish a Messianic Kingdom of worldwide influence. And they also reject many of the prophecies in their own Scriptures.

This does not mean that Reform Jews are not interested in the nation of Israel today. They send money, and they send help. They do all they can for the nation's support and aid, and they do this for humanitarian reasons. But the fact that today there is a nation of Israel providentially restored and protected has become a good reason for uneasiness by some Reform Jews. Because of some of the events that have happened, a number of the Reform have stopped

13. Those Christians who adhere to a premillennial eschatology will agree with them. We have never seen it to fail that when Jewish people realize there are Christians who believe in a literal restoration of Israel, they are startled and surprised. Many times this point of view will build a bridge of understanding to Jewish hearts. (See the appendix to this chapter.)

in their theological tracks and have looked to the other side of the theological spectrum.

In recent statements Reform Judaism has recognized the Zionist movement but still does not accept a personal Messiah. We can hope and pray that, as we share our faith with Reform Jews, the Word of God will commend its relevancy and prophetic authority. The Bible does have answers for the problems of the day and states very clearly that only God can institute the Kingdom. Man will never do it.

ESCHATOLOGY

Eschatology is the doctrine of the last things. Insofar as the Orthodox and the Conservative are concerned, the great emphasis is not in the end things or what is to happen to the soul after death or the nature of the resurrection and the judgment. This does not mean that tradition has nothing to say about these things; there are many opinions about eschatology. But it must be remembered that the great emphasis is on the importance of learning how to live here and now by good morals and ethics rather than on the future.

Reform Judaism also puts very little or no stress on eschatology. Death ends all, according to most Reform Jews, except for the memory of the departed treasured by the living. If there is any eternal life, it is what the living carry in their minds and in their hearts concerning the life and deeds of the departed. For that reason, when we talk about intermediate state, resurrection, and ultimate destiny, there is practically a blank on the Reform side.

The Orthodox and the Conservative beliefs in this area contain many opinions and views. The Hebrew Scriptures speak of a person going to Sheol in the intermediate state (the period between his death and the resurrection). According to the traditions, in general, the righteous go to one side of Sheol and the unrighteous go to the other. Between the two areas is a wide chasm, and there is no passage from one side to the other. Again, however, there is a variety of opinions, so there is no one defined view as to precisely what happens to the person in the intermediate state.

In consideration of the resurrection there are also differences of ideas. Some believe in a universal resurrection in which everyone will be raised with a physical body from the dead. Others say only departed Israelites will be raised. Still others believe that only the righteous, both Jew and Gentile, will be raised. There is a general belief in a resurrection of physical bodies, but as to the nature of the body there is no unanimity at all. According to the one view, resurrection is of the same body in which one was buried, while another holds that the raised body is a restored body almost equivalent to a glorified body.

Some believe that, as the ultimate destiny, the righteous will enjoy God in a number of places after the period of the Messianic Kingdom. There are many names given to these places. The different places are graded to reflect degrees of perfection and rewards achieved by the righteous.

Concerning the future of the unrighteous, three main views are expressed. Some indicate the unrighteous will suffer for a while; and when they repent, they will be released from suffering and enter into the presence of God. One opinion actually says that the unrighteous merely need to repent in the place of torment, and then they will be ejected from this place, like an arrow out of a bow, to land in the presence of God. Others state that the unrighteous suffer for a while and then are annihilated; they simply cease to exist. And then there is the view that the unrighteous suffer forever. The majority probably hold the first view, that there is to be a universal salvation after a period of suffering.

Eschatology can be a very intriguing topic of conversation. What a precious privilege it is to share our assured hope of eternal life which the Messiah gives to the believer! What a joy it is to tell of the certainty in our hearts that when we leave this life we shall enjoy the presence of God forever! No wonder one of Israel's choicest Messianic Jews declared, recognizing and acknowledging the Messiah, "I am hard pressed from both directions, having the desire to depart and be with Christ [Messiah]" (Phil 1:23)! This was no morbid desire to die, nor did it reflect a lack of concern for the needs of his generation or for the problems of those to whom he ministered. The whole context of the first chapter of Philippians indicates his genuine, heartfelt concern for the people of his day. But Paul faced the reality that someday he would die, and therefore he gave priority to his own spiritual needs. We must all secure our vertical relationship with God through the Messiah and His righteousness to enter in and become a part of God's family. Having done this, there is that blessed confidence and hope of entrance into the eternal sphere of life after this life. The one who shirks the responsibility of heeding the Word of God and the claims of the Messiah does this only with the danger of an eternal separation from God. As Jewish people and Christians share their faiths, ours is the privilege of sharing a priceless experience that has eternal consequences with the Jewish people—the Lord's kinsmen after the flesh.

APPENDIX

A pastor of a church on the north side of Chicago, where there are many Jewish people, once had a unique Sunday-afternoon service to demonstrate his interest and that of his church in the future of the land of Israel. He advertised throughout the community that there was going to be a special emphasis on Israel and that after the meeting there would be an offering received for the planting of trees in Israel. In addition to church folk, sixty Jewish people attended that meeting. During the service, the pastor preached a message on what he believed God had in mind for the nation of Israel: God was going to restore that nation, and the Word of God said that trees would be planted in the last days and would grow (Ez 34:27; 36:30, 35). He, as a Christian minister, was interested in the welfare and future of Israel, and this was the reason he was asking for an offering on behalf of Israel for trees. After the meeting, the church people and the Jewish folk had an opportunity to fellowship together over coffee and become acquainted. These Jewish people felt welcome when they saw the interest of this church and pastor on behalf of Israel. The heartfelt concern of that pastor became known throughout the Jewish community. Subsequent to this meeting, the pastor had many opportunities to address different kinds of Jewish groups.

We often wonder how we can reach the Jewish heart. The answer is through love, concern, and the desire to share what the Scriptures have to say to our Jewish friends.

DOCTRINES OF JUDAISM

NOTE: The Orthodox and Conservative beliefs are shown together because the two groups hold the same basic doctrines, although they differ in their practice of Judaism.

	Orthodox and Conservative	Reform
SCRIPTURES	Are given great emphasis and regarded as from God (Maimonides, Principles 6-9).	Are not verbally inspired in Bible sense.
	Torah is inspired in degrees.	Torah has errors but does stress an ethic and derives a moral.

ORAL LAW	Is the traditional understanding of the Scriptures and is stressed.	Is highly regarded but not considered authoritative.
		Is questioned through rational approach.
GOD	Concept is based upon Deuteronomy 6:4 (Maimonides, Principles 1-5).	Is regarded in monotheistic way; has great emphasis. (But is the belief personal?)
1) TRINITY	Is denied.	Is denied.
2) HOLY SPIRIT	Is recognized.	Their understanding varies.
MAN		
1) NATURE	Has good and evil bent.	Has divine spark.
2) POTENTIAL	Is greatly emphasized.	Is stressed.
3) FALL	Death is result of Adam's sin, but there is no original sin.	Not accepted; man is a product of evolution.
SIN	Is given great emphasis.	Is recognized.
	Horizontal stress (man to man) is major.	Social aspects are emphasized.
	Some vertical aspects (man to God) are present.	
SALVATION (JEWISH IDEA)	Is given strong emphasis.	Is seen as the social emphasis for this life.
	The great three are essential:	

	Prayer—*T*e*fillah*
	Good Works—
	  Miṣvot
	Repentance—
	  *T*e*shuvah*	

	Suffering has merit.	

MESSIAH	Is regarded as personal.	Personal Messiah is denied.
	Is seen as human or superhuman (but not God). Many Conservative believe as the Reform.	They are looking for Messianic golden age.
MESSIANIC KINGDOM	Has strong emphasis.	Is denied. Most are interested in fitting into current culture, but some have second thoughts.
	Day of judgment of the nations is to come.	
	Messiah will rectify all injustices.	
	Israel will be at the head of the nations.	
ESCHATOLOGY	Has little emphasis. It is more important to learn how to live here and now.	Has little emphasis.
		Death ends all except memory of the departed in the living.
	There are so many opinions that it is hard to define an ordered eschatology.	
1) INTERMEDIATE STATE*	Righteous have their place in Garden of Eden in Sheol.	
	Unrighteous have their place in Gehenna.	

*The time period between death and resurrection.

2) RESURREC-   Some rabbis indicate
TION   a universal one.

                    Some say only Israel.

                    Some say only the
                    righteous.

                    Is seen as physical.

                    Some believe the
                    body will be the same
                    body which was bur-
                    ied. Others say that
                    it will be renewed but
                    not glorified.

3) ULTIMATE   Righteous will enjoy
STATE   God in the Garden of
                    Eden.

                    For the unrighteous
                    there are different
                    ideas:

                    a) suffering, then
                       all saved (most
                       rabbis believe
                       this).

                    b) suffering, then
                       annihilation.

                    c) suffering for-
                       ever.

FOR FURTHER STUDY

BOOKS

Bamberger, B. J. *The Bible, a Modern Jewish Approach*. New
    York: Schocken, 1967.
———. *The Story of Judaism*. New York: Schocken, 1965.
Cohen, A. *Everyman's Talmud*. London: Dent, 1932.
———. *The Teaching of Maimonides*. London: Routledge,
    1919.
Cohon, S. S. *A Way of Life*. New York: Schocken, 1965.

Epstein, L. *The Jews, Their History, Culture, and Religion.* 2 vols. New York: Harper, 1955.

Gartenhaus, J. *Unto His Own.* Atlanta: Internat. Brd. of Jewish Missions, 1965. This basic handbook on Jewish beliefs was written by a Messianic Jew.

Ginsberg, L. *On Jewish Law and Lore.* Philadelphia: Jewish Publ. Soc. of Amer., 1955.

Heydt, H. *Studies in Jewish Evangelism.* New York: Amer. Brd. of Missions, 1951. Heydt, a Gentile Christian, is sensitive to the Jewish mind and has a depth of understanding of the Jewish heart.

Kac, A. *Spiritual Dilemma of the Jewish People.* Chicago: Moody, 1963. Kac, an outstanding Messianic Jew and former president of the Hebrew Christian Alliance, was a prolific writer on Israel of today.

Kohler, L. *Old Testament Theology.* London: Lutterworth, 1957.

Mattuck, I. *Essentials of Liberal Judaism.* London: Routledge, 1947.

Schechter, S. *Some Aspects of Rabbinic Theology.* New York: Behrman, 1936. Schechter, a distinguished Jewish scholar, was one of the guiding lights of Conservative Judaism in America.

Steinberg, M. *Basic Judaism.* New York: Harcourt, Brace & World, 1947. This is a compact presentation of Jewish beliefs by an author who is fair and objective toward all groups.

FILMSTRIPS

Judaism. Life Filmstrips. New York: Time-Life.

Judaism: Orthodox, Conservative, and Reform. New York: Bnai Brith. This is distributed by the Bnai Brith, 315 Lexington Avenue, New York, N.Y. 10016.

Judaism Today. Chicago: Soc. for Visual Ed.

Torah in Jewish Life. New York: Jewish Ed. Com. of N.Y.

FILMS

This Is Our Faith. Jewish Chatauqua Soc., 1955.

6

THE USE OF THE PROPHETIC MESSAGE IN FAITH SHARING

INTEREST IN PROPHECY

Prophecy has become an important topic in our day. Interest in future events is demonstrated by the strong attraction the occult holds for many. People are trying to peer into the future by all kinds of means in order to determine what is to come.

However, biblical prophecy is not dabbling with the occult to discover some information. The apologetic evidence of biblical prophecy is legitimate, God-given information that is 100-percent correct.[1] There are no scores of 60-40 percent accuracy as with the predictions of people labeled as prophets today. Long ago God laid down the ground rules for identifying bona fide prophets so the reliability of their utterances could be guaranteed (Deu 18:21-22).

The accuracy of the Scriptures in depicting future events should lead one to respect what the Word of God has to say. Generally, this evidence can be used with those who are

---

1. I am well aware that many Christians do not agree with some of the assertions made or positions taken in this chapter. This chapter is included because the approach to faith sharing by the means of national prophecy has often been an opportunity for a good discussion of what the Scriptures teach concerning the future of Israel. If the reader does not accept these prophetic views, I beg his indulgence. Our main concern in this chapter is to aid in understanding and sharing with our Jewish friends and not to major on differences among Christians in understanding prophecy.

agnostic or atheistic. Biblical prophecy is particularly important in that it calls attention to how much God is interested in His people Israel; and if we examine biblical prophecy carefully, it will reveal the purpose for human history, with the nation of Israel as the fulcrum of that history.

DEFINITION OF PROPHECY

Prophecy is a declaration of future events which no human wisdom or foresight is sufficient to make. God's foreknowledge includes knowing the countless contingencies of human affairs; and such knowledge is possible only within the omniscience of God. Therefore, by its very nature, prophecy must be *divine* revelation. In other words, true prophecy is never of human invention. Peter tells us this in 2 Peter 1:20-21. Prophecy depends on full knowledge of the many relationships of human affairs. Such knowledge and its communication in part is possible only to the all-knowing God. The contingencies of circumstances are intertwined in such a way that only an all-wise and all-knowing God could be able to supply us with the knowledge of events and situations before they take place.

PLACE OF PROPHECY IN SCRIPTURE

The place of prophecy in the Hebrew Scriptures is given in Deuteronomy 18:9-22; in the Mosaic constitution God gave the whole basis for the prophetic ministry of the Scriptures. Furthermore, He gave the tests whereby prophets could be examined as to whether they are true or false. Here is the value of what are called the short-range prophecies. For example, if a man said, "I'm a prophet," how were people to know he was a true prophet? His reliability was based on his short-range prophecies. If these prophecies were borne out everytime, then his audience was bound to listen to him. Jeremiah provides an example of a short-range prophecy in his confrontation with one of the false prophets of his day:

CONFRONTATION

> Then Hananiah the prophet took the yoke from the neck
> of Jeremiah the prophet and broke it. And Hananiah
> spoke in the presence of all the people, saying, "Thus says
> the LORD, 'Even so will I break within two full years, the
> yoke of Nebuchadnezzar king of Babylon from the neck
> of all the nations.' " Then the prophet Jeremiah went his
> way.
>
> And the word of the LORD came to Jeremiah, after
> Hananiah the prophet had broken the yoke from off the
> neck of the prophet Jeremiah, saying, "Go and speak to
> Hananiah, saying, 'Thus says the LORD, "You have broken
> the yokes of wood, but you have made instead of them
> yokes of iron." For thus says the LORD of hosts, the God of
> Israel, "I have put a yoke of iron on the neck of all these
> nations, that they may serve Nebuchadnezzar king of
> Babylon; and they shall serve him. And I have also given
> him the beasts of the field" ' " (Jer 28:10-14) .

SHORT-RANGE PROPHECY

> Then Jeremiah the prophet said to Hananiah the proph-
> et, "Listen now, Hananiah, the LORD has not sent you, and
> you have made this peope trust in a lie. Therefore thus
> says the LORD, 'Behold, I am about to remove you from
> the face of the earth. This year you are going to die, be-
> cause you have counseled rebellion against the LORD' "
> (vv. 15-16) .

FULFILLMENT

> So Hananiah the prophet died in the same year in the
> seventh month (v. 17) .

The false prophet prophesied a good message for Israel,
but Jeremiah said there had been no good message. Jeremiah told the false prophet, "You will be dead within a
year," and Hananiah died in two months (vv. 1 and 17) .
This short-range prophecy established the validity of the
genuine prophet and gave further credence to his long-

range predictions. By the way, these are valid tests for those today who claim to be able to prophesy.

We do have the means to share with our Jewish friends an inerrant Word that very carefully depicts the inception of a nation, describes their fortunes down through history, and also describes very carefully some of the future events concerning the Jewish people.

THE ABRAHAMIC COVENANT

We can permit God's Word to speak to us and our Jewish friends concerning the Abrahamic Covenant, a very significant prophecy. This covenant can be used to answer objections by many of our secularized Jewish friends. They may question the validity of biblical prophecy in an attempt to hide their Jewish identity, but the Abrahamic Covenant relates beautifully to the inception of the Jewish people as well as their continued presence among the community of nations.

THE STATEMENT

The statement of the covenant is given in Genesis 17:2, "And I will establish My covenant between Me and you." This was announced around 2000 B.C.E., more than four thousand years ago.

THE TERMS

Now notice the terms of this covenant. The first is that Abraham was promised a great number of offspring: "And I will multiply you exceedingly. . . . I will make you exceedigly fruitful" (Gen 17:2, 6). The second term is that many nations and peoples would owe their existence to Abraham: "And you shall be the father of a multitude of nations. . . . For I will make you the father of a multitude of nations. . . . And I will make nations of you, and kings shall come forth from you" (Gen 17:4-6). Abraham is depicted here as the father of a multitude of nations. Today, many peoples, including the Arabs, regard him as their progenitor.

Still another term is seen: "And I will establish My covenant between Me and you and your descendants after you throughout their generations for an everlasting covenant, to be a God to you and to your descendants after you" (Gen 17:7). Notice that this covenant, confirmed to Isaac (Gen 17:19, 21) and later to Jacob (Gen 25:23; 35:9-15), was given by God to guarantee historical continuity for Abraham's descendants through Isaac and through Jacob down to the present day. It is because of divine protection in honor of a promise that Abraham's descendants, particularly the Jewish people, have continued to this day.

We can share with our Jewish friends that this is why Jewish people have existed to this day. Agnostic Jews might want to disclaim their background, but God Himself will not permit the assimilation, amalgamation, or disappearance of the seed of Abraham through Isaac and Jacob. In other words, it is not because of any human strength or ingenuity that Jewish people are a part of the modern scene. God has always protected them as a people and continues to do so. God has kept them for some four thousand years on the basis of a covenant whereby He has guaranteed their continuance. As long as there is a history of the human race, there will be a Jewish people.

Still another term is an everlasting and irrevocable title to a definite piece of real estate, a title to a land. God announced to Abraham: "On that day the LORD made a covenant with Abram saying, 'To your descendants I have given this land, from the river of Egypt as far as the great river, the river Euphrates'" (Gen 15:18). As long as there is a history of the human race, the seed of Abraham through Isaac and Jacob has the title deed to the land within the boundaries described in this passage.[2] This has not yet

2. This does not mean that Abraham's other descendants do not have their place in the Middle East. In a very loose way, the Scriptures

been fulfilled in its entirety, but it serves as the biblical basis for the right to the land that Jewish people claim. It is a claim grounded in the Word and promise of God. No other land will suffice for the Jewish people. If the Jew is not at home on this plot of land, then what other area does he call home? During centuries of wandering, Jewish people have always been reminded at Passover, "This year, here; next year, in Jerusalem."

Note that the covenant is unconditional in character. God took the initiative and instituted this covenant. It is not dependent on people's obedience, as is the Mosaic covenant. God said, "I establish my covenant between Me and you," and it remains in force to this day.

THE DAVIDIC COVENANT

In a further emphasis upon the validity of the Word of God, His promise, we turn our attention to another covenant known as the Davidic covenant.

THE STATEMENT

Notice the statement given in 2 Samuel 7:12-13: "I will raise up your descendant after you . . . and I will establish his kingdom. . . . I will establish the throne of his kingdom forever." This word was proclaimed about 1000 B.C.E., a thousand years after the word to Abraham.

do describe the dwelling places of Abraham's sons (Gen 25:6). When Abraham settled the inheritance rights of his six sons, he sent them away to the land of the East. This is a very loose way of describing the area, but we can assume that after having spelled out the inheritance of the line of Isaac and Jacob, the rest of the Middle East was to be for the sons of Ishmael and Esau as well as the descendants of Abraham's six sons by his second wife, Keturah. In time, the latter intermarried and became what we know today as the Arab peoples, with their place in the Middle East along with Jacob's sons.

I do not intend to enter into the modern dispute concerning the problems of refugees, property settlements, or rights to land except to carefully exegete the Scripture. What we can say concerning the modern scene is that the Balfour Declaration, upheld by the old League of Nations and the present United Nations, asserted the right of Jewish people to live in their homeland in the Middle East.

THE TERMS

We now examine the terms. The first is that the house and throne of David are everlasting: "I will establish the throne of his kingdom forever" (2 Sa 7:13). David was surprised by this information (2 Sa 7:18), but as in the approach to Abraham, God initiated the promises guaranteeing the surety of the house and throne of David. We need to recognize that, even when the historical kingdom is interrupted (for example, when Israel had no king after the Babylonian exile, and later on when Israel had no priesthood or temple after 70 C.E.), other promises indicate that this throne will yet be revived and a member of the house of David will occupy it.

We understand now that this One of David's illustrious house is David's greater Son, the Messiah.[3] The New Testament identifies Jesus as the Messiah and King in Matthew 22:41-46 where Jesus discussed the issue with the religious leaders of Israel. Even though Jesus died to provide the atonement for our sins and to fulfill the exchange-of-life principle, this was not to be the end of the Messianic Kingdom on earth. The Messianic Kingdom—that is, the Kingdom over which Messiah Jesus of the house of David will yet reign—will yet be an established Kingdom on earth (Ac 1:6-7).

This information is always startling, especially to Jewish young people. The state of Israel today is a representational democracy, organized along socialist lines. But God's plan is yet to materialize in a future Kingdom in which the Messiah will reign as a benevolent but firm King. This King and Kingdom will be according to God's promise and choice, and the Messiah will govern in this theocratic Kingdom with full authority.

3. See chap. 8. However, many of the more theologically liberal Conservatives do not believe that a personal Messiah will come to institute the Messianic Kingdom. Along these lines, many are like the Reform Jews.

Still another term of this covenant is its unconditionality. As in the Abrahamic covenant, God appeared and made a pronouncement. In a sense, then, the Davidic covenant operates simultaneously with the Abrahamic. The promises which guarantee the continuity of the Jewish people concomitantly indicate a Messianic Kingdom and a King who will reign over these very people when the proper time arrives.

Tracing Jewish History and Prophecy

To understand properly the terms of the covenants worked out within history, we need to review some history (see chap. 1). This is necessary in order to properly relate to the covenants within the context of history.

Israel became, through the centuries, the people of the wandering foot. Moses had said, "And among these nations you shall find no rest, and there shall be no resting place for the sole of your foot; but there the LORD will give you a trembling heart, failing of eyes, and despair of soul (Deu 28:65). The whole passage must be read (Deu 28: 62-68) in this matter of a wandering people described so graphically thousands of years ago by the most highly revered figure in Jewish history.

A Persecuted People

Israel, throughout the centuries, has been a persecuted people. This has already been pointed out, for example, in their experiences in the Babylonian exile, the intertestamental period, and particularly in the period of church history beginning with the fourth century (see chap. 2). Some of the pages of Church history are black indeed in the matter of Church-Jewish relationships: the aftermath of Chrysostom's anti-Jewish homilies, the experiences of the Crusades, and the Eastern European horrors are only a few of the oppressions.

FINAL DEVASTATION

The prophetic events yet to happen are painful to relate. There was a tremendous victory for the Israelis in the 1967 conflict, and at the end of the Yom Kippur conflict the Israelis had captured additional territory; but that is not the end of conflict in the Middle East. Jesus referred to the abomination of desolation (Mt 24:15) and also to a "great tribulation, such as has not occurred since the beginning of the world until now, nor ever shall" (Mt 24:21). This prophecy is yet to be fulfilled, since nothing in recorded history fulfills it.

There are Hebrew Scriptures that refer to the future of Israel. Jeremiah spoke of the time of Jacob's trouble (Jer 30:7), a time which is yet to come.[4] How much trouble? In Zechariah 13:8-9 we note,

> "It will come about in all the land," declares the LORD, "That two parts in it will be cut off and perish; but . . . I will bring the third part through the fire, refine them as silver is refined, and test them as gold is tested."

It is difficult to imagine this carnage, and it ought to bring tears to the eyes of every child of God. We wish our Israeli friends well as they seek to rebuild the land, but this is what is yet ahead. The pressure by various power blocks who will move into the Middle East (and we see the beginnings of this today) will bring this tribulation upon Israel.[5]

4. Some scholars might feel that the past experiences of the Jewish people could very well be the Jacob's trouble prophesied. Yet, the Scripture speaks of the *land*, and whenever a reference is made to the land, it always is a reference to the land of Israel. In other words, the Scriptures are speaking of a holocaust in the land itself, not any other place.
5. The prophetic Scriptures speak of three major power blocks that will figure prominently in the end times; the locations of the blocks are always given in relation to the land of Israel. There is a northern block that will move down into the land (Eze 38:15; 39:2); there is an eastern block that will come into the Middle East in the end of days (Rev 16:12); and there is to be a reconstituted western block of European nations. It seems that we are in the days when these power blocks could become embroiled in the Middle East and little Israel will be in the middle of it.

There are dark days of intense, worldwide anti-Jewishness ahead for the nation of Israel.

THE COMING OF THE MESSIAH

Thank God, He will preserve the people of Israel in the midst of all this destruction. But He preserves them for a purpose. The day will come when, out of desperate conditions, a remnant will call upon the Lord for deliverance. The Hebrew Scriptures declare, "They will call on My name, and I will answer them; I will say, 'They are My people,' and they will say, 'The LORD is my God' " (Zech 13:9*b*). It is then that the Messiah will come to deliver them (Zech 14:4).

It is extremely interesting to note how the prophet describes the identity of the Messiah:

> And I will pour out on the house of David and upon the inhabitants of Jerusalem the Spirit of grace and of supplication, so that they will look on Me whom they have pierced; and they will mourn for Him, as one mourns for an only son, and they will weep bitterly over Him, like the bitter weeping over a first-born (Zech 12:10).

The rest of the chapter describes the whole nation in mourning for this Deliverer.

This has always been regarded as a Messianic passage. The Orthodox Jews and many Conservatives are looking for the coming of the Messiah. But who is that particular One who comes? The One who delivers the nation, both physically and spiritually, is described as the One whom they have pierced. So great will be the shock of the generation of Israelis who behold His coming and view Him as the pierced One, that they go into a national lament. They will experience a bitterness of soul, as if repenting in bitter tears, because of the startling revelation that the deliverer

---

We might point out that aspects of the Rabbinic position teach that, just before the coming of the Messiah, there will be a period known as the foot of the Messiah when there will be a terrible conflagration on earth.

is the One who had been pierced for their sins when He was in Israel the first time. All is forgiven, however, in the face of a new set of conditions.[6]

As the Spirit of God is poured out on a new generation of Israelis, the nation experiences a spiritual rebirth. The result of this rebirth is that everyone will know the Lord, and the New Covenant will be made with Israelis because of a new spiritual relationship. It is the Messiah, no longer a lowly individual but a mighty monarch, who then effects this New Covenant. God's word can be considered so accurate in view of how He has never let His people Israel pass off the scene entirely.

THE NEW COVENANT

When the Spirit of grace is poured out and the nation is born again, there will then be the ratification of the New Covenant.

THE STATEMENT

The statement by God to the prophet Jeremiah, about 600 B.C.E., asserts,

> "Behold, days are coming," declares the LORD, "when I will make a new covenant with the house of Judah, not like the covenant which I made with their fathers in the day I took them by the hand to bring them out of the land of Egypt, My covenant which they broke. . . . But this is the covenant which I will make" (Jer 31:31-33).

---

6. After the First century C.E., Talmudic thought developed the concept of two Messiahs, one the son of Joseph and the other the son of David. The son of Joseph will be involved in the terrible world upheaval in the days before the Messianic Kingdom is instituted, but he will die in all the fighting. After this period, the son of David, the Messiah, will then institute the Kingdom. In answer, we might indicate that this was not at all the thinking of the earlier rabbis in asserting the idea of two Messiahs. In addition, the Zechariah 12 passage emphasizes that it is a once-wounded Messiah who comes to deliver the people of Israel and set up the Kingdom; there is no evidence here that He dies in the attempt. He remains the mighty Conqueror who delivered His people.

As we saw, God will take the initiative to institute this compact at the proper time.

THE TERMS

Note some of the terms of this new covenant. First, this covenant—known also as Jeremiah's new covenant—is entirely new. It is *not* the old Mosaic covenant. It is "not like the covenant which I made with their fathers in the day I took them by the hand to bring them out of the land of Egypt" and which was broken by the people. It was the Mosaic covenant that was broken, not the Abrahamic covenant.[7] The Abrahamic covenant never was broken and never will be broken within a historical context of man's existence on earth. This new covenant will be a new agreement completely and is known as Jeremiah's new covenant.

The second of these terms treats the moral and spiritual condition of the people. Note that God says,

> "I will put My law within them, and on their heart I will write it; and I will be their God, and they shall be My people. And they shall not teach again, each man his neighbor and each man his brother, saying, 'Know the LORD,' for they shall all know Me, from the least of them to the greatest of them," declares the LORD, "for I will forgive their iniquity, and their sin I will remember no more" (Jer 31:33-34).

Here are moral and spiritual promises still to come in the

7. The Orthodox and the more conservative of the Conservative Jews speak of once again bringing the nation of Israel under the Mosaic Law, or covenant. It must be emphasized that the Mosaic constitution consists of three parts: the moral (Ten Commandments), the sacrificial (Temple ritual), and the legal. All these were bound into a unit and called the Mosaic covenant. If we take away any one of these parts, there can be no Mosaic covenant. Therefore, when the Temple was destroyed in 70 C.E., there could no longer be a Mosaic covenant. Even if the religious manage to erect some kind of Temple in Israel again, it will be short-lived because of the coming holocaust. The Mosaic covenant has been superseded by the spiritual blessings of Jeremiah's new covenant in our age today and by the totality of spiritual and material blessings of Jeremiah's new covenant in the Messianic Kingdom to come (see fn. 9 of this chap.).

course of history to the nation of Israel as well as to the
whole world. Here are a people regenerated by the ministry of the Spirit of God on behalf of the remnant (Zech
12:10). This covenant will not be completely consum-
mated with the nation until Zechariah 13:8-9 and 12:10
take place in history. Clearly, a literal fulfillment of this
passage is still future.

The third term of this new covenant guarantees it by the
very order and stability of the created universe: " 'If this
fixed order departs from before Me,' declares the LORD,
'then the offspring of Israel also shall cease from being a
nation before Me for ever' " (Jer 31:36).[8] If man's knowledge is ever so advanced that he can measure the heavens
above or search out the foundations of the earth, there will
then be a case for the dismissal of Israel as a people (v. 37).
Clearly the illustrations are given to emphasize that God's
purposes are so intertwined with His people Israel that in
order for Him to end the existence of Israel among the nations of men, He would have to cancel the very laws that
govern the operation of the cosmos. The implications are
that men will never be able to thwart God's intended purpose concerning His people Israel.

Still another term emphasizes that this whole future situation is within a historical context. This covenant is made
with a literal, regathered people, Israel (Jer 31:10-12), with
a people on earth who will live in a restored and expanded
city of Jerusalem (vv. 38-40). Here is the distinction be-

8. A proper exegesis of the Jeremiah passage shows that verses 31-40
speak of the covenant. When we apply this covenant to the whole
nation, we cannot break up this passage. Verses 35-37 indicate that
the covenant is to be applied to a people that will never disappear
from the face of the earth as long as there is a history of the human
race. Verses 38-40 describe Jerusalem's extension northward and
westward. All of this is to be in a day when Israel will be brought
back and redeemed (vv. 10-11), in a day when the land will be
productive beyond measure (v. 12), and when Judah (or, Israel) will
be burgeoning with cities (v. 24). This is not to be applied to the
exiles from Babylon, since no new covenant was made with those
returnees. No, the application is for the future in the day when the
Messianic Kingdom will be instituted.

tween Jeremiah 31:31-40 and Hebrews 8:8-12.[9] In the Hebrews passage (as well as Ephesians 2:14b) the totality of *spiritual* blessings that come to both Gentile and Jewish persons when they recognize and receive Jesus as Saviour and Redeemer is realized. Spiritual *and material* blessings—the full promises of the Jeremiah passage—are reserved for the literal nation of Israel (and Gentiles who likewise believe) in the future, when the remnant in Israel recognize Jesus as their Messiah—the event prophesied in Zechariah 13:8-9; 12:10-14.

EFFECTS OF THE NEW COVENANT

The biblical presentation of the redemption of Israel shows a Messianic Kingdom presided over by the Messiah (Zech 14:8-9, 16; Ps 2:7-8); universal peace and disarmament (Is 2:4); rectification of social problems (Is 65:21-22); solutions of the problems of diversity of religions, as the Messiah receives all worship (Zech 6:12-13; 14:16); cessation of physical disease and deformity (Is 35:5-6); and animal natures changed to be at peace with themselves and mankind (Is 11:6-8).

The effects are particularly noted in Isaiah 2:1-4. Isaiah the prophet wrote these lines about 700 B.C.E., and yet we are aware of the freshness of his appeal for the day in which we live. We also rejoice in the future promise of the prophecy, "He will judge between the nations" (Is 2:4), where the Messiah will render a righteous judgment among the nations of the earth. Furthermore, He will "render decisions for many peoples; and they will hammer their swords into plowshares, and their spears into pruning hooks.

9. The difference between Jeremiah 31:31-40 and Hebrews 8:8-12 is clarified when we compare these two passages. We immediately note that only verses 31-34 from Jeremiah are used in Hebrews. This is the emphasis on the spiritual and moral aspects of the New Covenant while the material aspects (vv. 35-40, 10-12 and v. 24) are omitted. We can conclude only that the spiritual aspects of Hebrews are to apply to this age, and the combination of spiritual and material blessings in the totality of Jeremiah's new covenant will yet apply in the fullness of the Messianic Kingdom.

Nation will not lift up sword against nation, and never again will they learn war" (Is 2:4). On the basis of this pronouncement, we can tell our Jewish friends that it is not the United Nations that will ultimately effect universal disarmament. It will be accomplished by the Messiah, reigning in and from Jerusalem, at the time when the new covenant is established. Then the nations will live at peace among themselves, Jerusalem will be the center of the world capitals, and nations will send their representatives to the house of Jacob to learn the ways of the Lord (Is 2: 2-3).

CONCLUSION

By using a few passages from the Bible, we have demonstrated the relevancy of prophecy to contemporary Israel. We see something of the accuracy of the Word of God, which speaks with unsurpassed knowledge of current and future events, although the Hebrew Scriptures were written thousands of years ago. When we share our faith with our Jewish friends through the medium of prophecy, we can very well exclaim, "Hasn't God given us a wonderful order in His Word? Hasn't God spelled out beforehand the fortunes of the people Israel? How in the world can anyone remain an agnostic? How can a Jewish person say it doesn't make any difference whether he's Jewish or not?" As Jewish people and Christians share their faith, we can say that God's plans certainly make a difference. The whole movement of history is tied to prophecy that expresses God's purposes. God's aims and goals are tied to His Word and related to Israel, as He accomplishes His desires through His people Israel. So, on the basis of His precise plan and purpose for this world, we can tell our Jewish friends, "We ought to read the Scriptures together and let it speak to both of us. We ought to know what the Scriptures say, for they are a valid source of information and command our respect."

FOR FURTHER STUDY

Books

Berkhof, L. *The Second Coming of Christ.* Grand Rapids: Eerdmans, 1953. This book on prophecy comes from a moderate, amillennial point of view.

Feinberg, Charles. *Israel in the Last Days.* Altadena, Calif.: Emeth, 1953. This well-known Messianic Jew was dean of Talbot Theological Seminary, La Mirada, California.

DeHaan, M. R. *The Jew and Palestine in Prophecy.* Grand Rapids: Zondervan, 1950.

Hamilton, Floyd. *The Basis of Millennial Faith.* Grand Rapids: Zondervan, 1942. This prophecy presentation is from a modified, Reformed Church point of view.

Gordis, R. *Poets, Prophets, and Sages.* Bloomington, Ind.: Indiana U., 1971. Gordis, a professor and Jewish leader, writes from the Jewish point of view, with his emphasis often upon deriving lessons in righteousness and justice from the prophets, rather than presenting a prophetic outlook for the future.

Heschel, Abraham. *The Prophets.* New York: Harper, 1969. Writing from a Jewish point of view, Heschel puts strong emphasis on ethics and mystical outlook.

Kac, A. W. *The Rebirth of the State of Israel: Is It of God or Men?* London: Marshall, Morgan & Scott, 1958. This prolific writer is a well-known Messianic Jew.

———. *The Death and Resurrection of Israel.* Baltimore: King, 1969.

Kohler, K. *Jewish Theology.* New York: Ktav, 1968. This classical presentation of Jewish thinking is from a topical point of view.

McClain, Alva. *The Greatness of the Kingdom.* Grand Rapids: Zondervan, 1959. McClain, former president of the Grace College and Theological Seminary, has undergirded his classical presentation well with Scripture.

Pieters, George N. H. *The Theocratic Kingdom.* 3 vols. Grand Rapids: Kregel, 1952. This is another classic.

Pentecost, J. D. *Things to Come.* Findlay, Ohio: Dunham, 1958. This is a detailed argument for the Messianic Kingdom.

Sale-Harrison, L. *The Remarkable Jew.* London: Pickering & Inglis, n.d.

Saphir, Adolph. *Christ and Israel.* London: Marshall, Morgan & Scott, 1911. Saphir was a Messianic Jew of a previous generation, but his work is still quite helpful.

Walvoord, John. *Israel in Prophecy.* Grand Rapids: Zondervan, 1962. This small, helpful volume puts Israel in proper perspective within biblical prophecy.

———. *The Millennial Kingdom.* Findlay, Ohio: Dunham, 1959. This provides excellent argument for the position of the millennial Kingdom.

Wilkenson, J. *God's Plan for the Jew.* London: Milkmay Mission, 1944. Wilkenson, a Gentile Christian, gives an excellent presentation of Israel in prophecy.

FILMS

Three Minutes to Twelve and *Israel, Twentieth-Century Miracle.* Chicago: Amer. Assoc. for Jewish Evang. These films may be obtained from the American Association for Jewish Evangelism, 5860 N. Lincoln, Chicago, Illinois 60659.

The Return. Dallas: Evang. Com. Research Fund.

7

HOW TO PRESENT MESSIANIC PROPHECY

THE APPROACH—THE QUESTION OF RECOGNITION

How can Israel's Messiah be recognized? If the Messiah were to appear today, what credentials should we expect of Him?

In faith sharing with our Jewish friends, we assume that we have established a friendly relationship with them and that we recognize their special identity and genuinely love them. We must also consider their concept of the Messiah. In our study of Jewish doctrine in chapter 5, we have seen that the Orthodox and the Conservatives, as a rule, believe that the Messiah is yet to come. They will be sure to say that He is human and perhaps superhuman, but they will deny that He is divine.

The Reform Jewish person denies the concept of any personal Messiah, and it may seem to be a closed subject. However, I have been able to share with my Reform Jewish friends our concepts of the Messiah because we want the Word of God to speak to both of us about Him. Recall Israel's confession, the Sh^ema (Deu 6:4): the first word is "Hear," and therefore we both want to *hear* what the Word of God has to say. Regardless of what Jewish persons believe, all ought to want to study the Scriptures.

Notice the use of the term *Messiah* rather than *Christ*. In chapter 2 on Church-Jewish relations, we noted some of the persecution and antiJewishness that has been carried on in the name of Christ. The term *Messiah* should be used, because our Jewish friends will not consider it offensive and it will convey a biblical presentation of the Anointed One, rather than some warped idea conveyed by the term *Christ* due to misguided actions against Jewish people.

Considering the differences between Jewish thought and the New Testament, how can the truth about the Messiah be determined? This is a good question to raise. It is the Word of God, the Hebrew Scriptures, which tells us how to recognize Israel's Messiah. Here we find the Messiah's credentials. And, as we let the Hebrew Scriptures speak to us, both Jewish people and Christians, we do not begin with talking about Jesus Christ. Eventually, we will need to identify the Messiah, but in the beginning we discuss the Messiah and emphasize His credentials.[1]

Hebrew Scriptures' Answer to the Question

We turn to what is known as the humiliation experiences of the Messiah. Jewish people who believe in a personal Messiah will be open to the presentation of an exalted Messiah of the lineage of David, who will rule as a great King and have all authority. What is important at first is to emphasize His earthly ministry, His person, and His work. Through this means we will eventually be able to identify the Messiah.

Birthplace

The Messiah was to be born in Bethlehem: "But as for you, Bethlehem Ephrathah, too little to be among the clans of Judah, from you One will go forth for Me to be ruler in Israel. His goings forth are from long ago, from the days of eternity" (Micah 5:2; 5:1 in the Hebrew Bible). We

---

1. In any sharing attempt, we never want to talk down to people, especially Jewish people. Since they too are a people of the Book, it is best to share with them so that the Word speaks to both of us.

have this information about the Messiah's birthplace. If He were to make His appearance today, we would have every right to ask the question, Where was He born? Was He born in Bethlehem?

MANNER OF BIRTH

We also note that the Hebrew Scriptures have something to say about the peculiarity of the Messiah: "Therefore the Lord Himself will give you a sign: behold, a virgin [the *'almah*—one should use the Hebrew here for the term that is translated "virgin" in the KJV, ASV, or NASB[2]] will be with child and bear a son, and she will call His name Immanuel" (Is 7:14). We do believe that the Messiah is virgin-born and feel that this is the correct translation of the term *'almah* when it is applied to the mother of the Messiah. But at this point we do not want to go off on a sidetrack with our Jewish friends on the meaning of *'almah* or whether or not the translation "virgin" is correct.

As the prophet himself declares, "the Lord Himself will give you a sign"; it is the word "sign" that is important for our discussion. What we want our friends to see is that the Messiah is brought forth in a peculiar manner, which is designated as "a sign." There is something miraculous about this one.

Furthermore, He is called "Immanuel," which means "God with us." When we note carefully what Micah 5:2 says, we see the unique nature of this Person. The Messiah is to be born in Bethlehem and to rule Israel, but the rest of the passage indicates "His goings forth are from long ago" or, literally, "whose existence has been from of old, from the days of eternity." Now clearly we have someone who truly is a miraculous sign: He is human in His birth in Bethlehem, but He has always existed, from eternity. The

2. The Jewish translation of *'almah* is "young woman," and our Jewish friends will contend for this translation.

Messiah is born as a human being, and yet He is also "God
with us."

TIME OF BIRTH

Another credential from the Scriptures, concerning the
time of Messiah's coming, can be derived from Daniel 9:
24-27; but this can result in a long, detailed discussion
about the "weeks" or "sevens." In sharing with a Jewish
person we do not want to get into something so involved
that he loses interest.

But there is another passage of Scripture that throws some
light on the time of the Messiah's coming. We read in Genesis 49:10, "The scepter shall not depart from Judah, nor
the ruler's staff [lawgiver] from between his feet, until
Shiloh comes, and to him shall be the obedience of the peoples." This has always been considered a Messianic passage,
with the term *Shiloh* being a synonym for *Messiah*. *Shiloh*
can mean literally, "which is unto him," or, "what pertains
or belongs to him;" therefore it forms a good description of
Messiah.

Here Jacob had an unusual message for Judah. He
prophesied that the rulers among the descendants of Judah
would not set aside their right to rule their people in the
future and not hand over the lawmaking power of the nation (later known as the Sanhedrin) to someone else, but
that the Messiah would come first. In other words, the
prophecy is that the Messiah would come before Judah
would turn over its governing and lawmaking power as a
united people and place it in Messiah's hands.[3]

To check this out from our vantage point today, we look
back to the tragic date of 70 c.e. and realize that after that
date in history Judah did lose its right to make laws and

---

3. Here again, some Christians will not accede to the prophetic views
   espoused at various points; and, as we indicated in the previous chapter, we beg the reader's indulgence. All Christians can subscribe to
   the main points in this chapter which can be used as we share our
   faith.

govern itself as a national entity. But this was because most of the nation did not acknowledge its King or the Kingdom Had they done so, they would have given the scepter and lawmaking power to Messiah after His atonement for sin, and the Messianic Kingdom would have begun. It is true that there have been bodies of scholars who subsequently brought together beliefs and traditions and put traditions down into writing, but this is not lawgiving in the same sense that the Sanhedrin was a lawgiver in the ranks of the nation, nor in the same sense that Judah has a scepter of rulership over a unified people. So we can share with our Jewish friends that the Messiah would have to come, from our perspective of history today, prior to what happened in the first century c.e., when Judah lost its nationhood and what pertained to it as a commonwealth.

No doubt, if our Jewish friend has a keen grasp of issues, he will by this time say, "Oh, you are talking about Jesus." In our faith sharing we can let him draw this conclusion on his own, but we will continue to permit the Hebrew Scriptures to speak of the Messiah, since there is more to say about how one recognizes the Messiah from His credentials in the Hebrew Scriptures.

HIS RECEPTION BY HIS PEOPLE

We turn our attention to the reception that the Messiah will receive from His people. Only two verses are indicated here, although there are many more in a similar vein:

> He was despised and forsaken of men, a man of sorrows, and acquainted with grief; and like one from whom men hide their face. He was despised, and we did not esteem Him. . . . But He was pierced through for our transgressions, He was crushed for our iniquities; the chastening for our well-being fell upon Him, and by His scourging we are healed (Is 5:3, 5) .

No doubt our Jewish friend will maintain that this passage refers to the nation of Israel. Israel's religious leaders today identify this entire passage with the nation and insist that the description of suffering applies to the experience of the Jewish people across the centuries.

The key to the whole problem of exegesis is in Isaiah 53: 10: a phrase there says, "when thou shalt make his soul an offering for sin" (KJV). The word used here for "offering," *'asham,* is the same word in Leviticus 5, where it means "trespass offering." When we go back into the Hebrew Scriptures and read about the qualifications for the trespass offering (or any offering), we find that these offerings were to be perfect, without spot or blemish. At this point, if our Jewish friend persists in saying that Isaiah 53 refers to the nation, we can raise the questions, Can you say that Israel is without spot or blemish—perfect in every way? Can Israel fulfill the qualifications of a trespass offering, or 'asham? Usually our Jewish friends will say no.[4] The conclusion is that Isaiah had in mind a unique, perfect individual, rather than the nation. We apply the passage in its entirety, therefore to an individual Messiah who is perfect.

Israel's ancient leaders always considered some of this chapter as referring to the Messiah as an individual who would rule His Kingdom in great power. They referred the descriptions of suffering to the nation as the suffering servant. The nation was bearing the message of God to the world, since they had the Torah; and this put them in the position of a lowly servant who might have to undergo persecution while performing his task. The viewpoint that the whole chapter refers to the nation did not fully develop until the Middle Ages. The Jewish leaders reacted under the impact of the testimony of many in the Church who used Isaiah 53 as a proof text for the Messiahship of Jesus. To es-

---

4. I recall a discussion of this passage with a rabbi. He reached for his Bible as we were discussing the qualifications of the offerings; he read in the Hebrew, pondered for a moment, then closed the Bible and said, "Let's not discuss this any further." We can very well observe that the truth of the point came home.

cape the implications of a suffering Messiah as the one who dies as a trespass offering, they omitted the more ancient concept of a personal Messiah reigning gloriously and taught that this passage in its entirety referred to the nation as the suffering servant.

If we look at the passage objectively enough, we will have to see the description of a person who, in a unique way, takes upon Himself our iniquities (Is 53:6). Thus, the Messiah is to suffer. He is to be despised and rejected by His own people as well as many other peoples.

DEATH OF THE MESSIAH

In Psalm 22:16 we read, "For dogs have surrounded me; a band of evildoers has encompassed me; they pierced my hands, and my feet." This is a Messianic psalm (it has always been regarded as such), and there is an amazing accuracy in what is proclaimed here. David wrote this Psalm about 1000 B.C.E., and in that day stoning was the method of capital punishment. David spoke of Messiah's hands and feet being pierced. Under the influence of the Spirit of God, he described a manner of execution that was foreign to the people of his day. The period in which crucifixion was the common mode of execution was hundreds of years future, in the time of the Romans, who used this peculiar method. Not only was the death described, but the rest of Psalm 22 relates the suffering accompanying His death.

I am well aware that the translation by Jewish people of Psalm 2:16 is "like a lion, my hands and my feet," instead of the term, "they pierced" and that many manuscripts support the reading adopted by Jewish people. However, the problem of translation rests upon the decision as to what the final consonant of the word might be. It would seem that, for purposes of the description of death, the main point is that the hands and feet become mangled. The whole psalm pictures a death scene in which people stand about while an individual is suffering and dying. There is nothing to militate against the mangling of the hands and feet that crucifixion produces, regardless of how one translates the message. In our faith sharing, this is another point on which we do not want to be sidetracked. The support for the interpretation of crucifixion is good, especially when substantiated by Zechariah 12:10, which unquestionably calls Messiah the pierced One.

THE MESSIAH'S COMING AGAIN

The Orthodox and many Conservatives believe in the Messiah who is yet to come. One excellent description is given in Zechariah 12:10, in which the prophet says, "And I will pour out on the house of David and on the inhabitants of Jersualem, the Spirit of Grace and of supplication, so that they will look on Me whom they have pierced; and they will mourn for Him, as one mourns for an only son, and they will weep bitterly over Him, like the bitter weeping over a first-born."

It is the Messiah's coming that is the occasion for God to pour out His grace and Spirit upon the people of Israel. Note carefully that when He comes, the people will recognize Him as the pierced One, and their reaction will be one of great lament, showing a broken heart.

Of course, our Jewish friend could say at this point, "You are talking about Jesus!" But let him draw his own conclusions, since we are not yet ready to make the identification. We will emphasize that there is the visible appearance of a marred body. The Jewish people, if they are taught to believe in a Messiah, are looking for a great conqueror.[5] The Scripture describes Messiah's coming as a great conqueror, but He upsets Israelis at His coming because He has in His body the wounds which He sustained in His first advent (see Zech 12:10, above). The generation that sees this is

---

5. As already noted, there are many Conservative Jewish people who do not believe in a personal Messiah. They hold that we all will bring in the Messianic Kingdom by our own efforts to change the world. They are similar to the Reform Jew on this doctrine.

horror-struck and mourns bitterly over the previous misconception and misidentification.

RELATIONSHIP BETWEEN MESSIAH AND JESUS OF NAZARETH

In our faith sharing we have said enough concerning the humiliation credentials of the Messiah. It seems that we are ready to say something about the identification.

We might ask the question, Of whom do the prophets speak? Usually when we have had opportunity to go through the credentials procedure, the response is, You are talking about Jesus Christ! Now that is exactly the point. If Jesus is not the Messiah, as Jewish people claim, then the Messiah must be someone who is *just like Jesus.* He must fulfill all the prophecies that we have mentioned (which are only a few of the many in the Hebrew Scriptures) that particularly emphasize the humiliation of the Messiah as He entered into human life and Jewish culture and encountered the people's response toward Him. Many more prophecies in the Hebrew Scriptures depict additional credentials which the Messiah must fulfill. So, if someone rejects the credentials of Jesus as the Messiah, then the Messiah will have to be another person similar to what is proclaimed in the New Testament concerning Jesus.

What are the possibilities for a repetition of circumstances in which a present or future Messiah could duplicate the earthly life and ministry of Jesus as witnessed and recorded by Jesus' contemporaries? Historically, it would be almost impossible to reset history in order to recreate the conditions which existed two thousand years ago. This would necessitate the birth of the Messiah in Bethlehem,[6] the rejection of such a Messiah by His people, the handing over of the rulership and lawmaking authority of a nation to a Messiah who had made an atonement, the death of such

6. It is interesting to note that there are no Jewish people living in Bethlehem today, since this is an Arab city. If this continues to be the case, a future fulfillment for Micah 5:2 will be a difficulty.

a Messiah, and the fulfillment of countless other prophecies. No, the only conclusion which our Jewish friends can draw is that the Hebrew Scriptures contain humiliation prophecies concerning the Messiah and that the New Testament accurately identifies Jesus as that Messiah. There can be no other interpretation of the historical data. A generation will someday recognize this, when He comes to deliver His people, bearing in His body the wounds He received in the days of His flesh. Our plea is that many of our Jewish friends today make the identification of Jesus as the Messiah and then go on to receive Him as the full atonement for sin.

SOME CLAIMS BY AND CONCERNING JESUS THE MESSIAH

Jesus made claims that transcend life's experiences as well as provide for a life beyond physical death. If He is the Messiah as He claimed to be, then we can expect such promises and pronouncements by and concerning Him. If He was not the Messiah, then such pronouncements would not be worth considering or accepting. In fact, they would be only the ideals of a misguided religious zealot or the ravings of someone out of his mind. That He was not regarded as demented can be attested by the thousands of Messianic Jews who followed Him in his own generation, to say nothing of the millions of people since the days of His flesh who have tested His claims and found them to be true. The following are only a few of the many claims He made.

LIFE

Jesus the Messiah claimed, "I came that they might have life, and might have it abundantly" (Jn 10:10). Jewish people especially love life and the zest of it. The abundant life that is ever possible has a dimension that is fulfilled only by Jesus' offer. The quality of the life that He proffers enables one to live victoriously and gloriously. It is that kind of life that can influence those around us as they observe the supernatural quality in it. The life is His very own, as already described in the concept of the exchange-of-life principle (see chap. 5).

But not only is there an abundant life here and now; there is also an eternal life in which one enjoys the presence of the Lord after this life ends. This eternal life also was offered by Jesus as a result of His ministry in His atonement for sin. When we recognize Him as the One who effected the full payment for our sins and appropriate this personally, we have eternal life. Someday, then, as a result of the barrier of sin being removed when we trust the atoning work of the Messiah on our behalf, we can enjoy the fellowship of God in His family forever.

CHANGE IN NATURE

In addition to offering an abundant life, Jesus the Messiah also claimed for those who believe in Him a basic change in nature. Paul indicates it: "Therefore if any man is in Christ [the Messiah], he is a new creature; the old things passed away; behold, new things have come" (2 Co 5:17). A belief in Jesus the Messiah results not in reform but in an actual, basic change in the heart; it is a complete change in the individual nature. It is a change which can affect the whole of society. As a result of this change, things which a man once loved, he now dislikes; the things which he once hated, he now loves. It is the kind of a change whereby the individual now has a deep concern for the needs of his fellowman and seeks to extend a helping hand. No mere religion can accomplish this revolution of character, but the living Messiah claims just such an accomplishment.

PEACE

Jesus the Messiah claimed that He was the One who could give the peace men so desperately crave. He said, "Peace I leave with you . . . not as the world gives, do I give to you. Let not your heart be troubled, nor let it be fearful" (Jn 14:27). More than anything, Jewish people crave peace, peace for themselves as individuals and peace for their nation. The place where peace starts is in the individual heart. Peace must first of all be the experience of the individual within himself. Jesus claimed to effect this very experience. The testimony of His true believers is that He makes good His claim. There can be the enjoyment of peace of heart, soul, and mind. When the individual is at peace with himself, he then can share his peace with those around him; and the influence goes on and on in an ever widening circle. When countless multitudes can experience this peace, the whole of society can then be changed.

EXCLUSIVE WAY TO GOD

Jesus the Messiah claimed to be the exclusive way to God: "I am the way, and the truth, and the life; no one comes to the Father, but through Me" (Jn 14:6). This was one of the most stupendous claims ever made. If an ordinary human being had made this assertion, one could say that it was the wild claim of some misguided man. But if this was an announcement by the real Messiah, then the claim has an urgent validity. Because of its implications, one must respond to this claim; a person's destiny is at stake. If one refuses to come to God this way, that is, through the Messiah, then he is like a thief, attempting to gain ends through unlawful means (Jn 10:1).

Jesus' claim to be the only way to the Father is not like those laws which can be repealed or changed—for example, traffic laws, or laws which change from generation to generation. Rather, His assertion is similar to the great, irrevocable laws of the universe—for example, the law of gravity and the laws governing the movement of the heavenly bodies. Jesus' announcement of this narrowness of way reflects the will of a sovereign God, who said that the experience of eternal life and entrance into His family is only through the Jewish Messiah. As we share our faith, it is to be hoped that many of our Jewish friends will avail themselves of this well-marked path.

CONCLUSION

Here is a challenge to our hearts to understand and to share the Messiah in this way with our Jewish friends. The challenge to each of us is that, as God gives us the opportunity, we share with our Jewish friends in this way and trust God for the response.

FOR FURTHER STUDY

Briggs, C. A. *Messianic Prophecy in the Old Testament.* New York: Scribners, 1886.

Cooper, David L. *The Eternal God Revealing Himself.* Harrisburg, Penn.: Evangelical Press, 1928. Cooper, a prolific writer of a past generation, has written extensively in this area.

———. *The God of Israel.* Los Angeles: Biblical Research, 1945.

Heinisch, Paul. "The Messiah." In *Theology of the Old Testament,* trans. Wm. Heidt. Colledgeville, Minn.: Liturgical Press, 1959. This book gives a Roman Catholic point of view with a good grasp on the biblical theology of the Hebrew Scriptures.

Huffman, J. A. *The Progressive Unfolding of the Messianic Hope.* New York: Doran, 1924.

Kligerman, A. J. *Messianic Prophecy in the Old Testament.* Grand Rapids: Zondervan, 1957. This Messianic Jew, a prolific writer of a generation ago, has a keen understanding of rabbinics and was a fearless proclaimer of the truth of the New Testament.

Lord, Eleazar. *The Messiah in Moses and the Prophets.* New York: Scribner, 1853. This is an old work but still excellent.

Ringgren, H. *The Messiah in the Old Testament.* Naperville, Ill.: Allenson, 1956. Ringgren's work demonstrates how the Messiah concept is handled from a critical point of view.

Sarachek, Joseph. *The Doctrine of the Messiah in Medieval Jewish Literature.* New York: Jewish Theological Sem., 1932.

8

BARRIERS TO COMMUNICATION

We are living in a day when there seems to be an openness among many Jewish people to discover for themselves, to examine the relationship of Jewish people to Jesus, and to hear the claims of the Church. But most Christians do not know how to communicate spiritual concepts to Jewish people, in spite of a number of denominational studies and the special endeavors of a few knowledgeable leaders. Attempts by Christians to relate to Jewish people could very well be hindered by misconceptions fostered by an unfortunate antagonism between the Church and the Jewish people (see chap. 2).

Even though the historical positions of the Church and of the Jewish people differ and their doctrinal positions overlap only at certain points, there exists a genuine and deep solidarity between the Church and Jewish people, because they revere the same Bible. It is a grievous hindrance to Jewish-Christian relationships that Christians have not recognized this solidarity. We are not speaking of a sentimental, humanitarian philo-Judaism, which Jewish people do not appreciate at all. Rather, there is a solidarity taught by the entire New Testament. In the New Testament we find common ground for faith sharing between Jewish people and Christians. If we do not acknowledge our Jewish heritage in the Scriptures, Jewish people will find it difficult to recognize the way of the Church, far less to walk in it.

Before we discuss the means of understanding, we need to treat some of the misconceptions Christians have about Jewish people. Then we shall proceed to some suggestions concerning language that will communicate best when sharing our common ground.

MISCONCEPTIONS

THE JEWS HAVE ALL THE MONEY

That all wealth is controlled by Jews is a well-worn cliché. Sometimes it is promoted by individuals who claim they know of wealthy Jewish business people in their hometown. But does this validate the claim? Is it true that Jews have all the money?

In answer, we must examine this claim more closely and get down to specifics. Of America's ten wealthiest families— including the Fords, Rockefellers, and DuPonts—not one is Jewish! Of America's four hundred wealthiest families, less than 10 percent are Jewish! Jewish people do not control the oil. (One of the richest Americans on earth, an oil man, J. Getty, was not Jewish.) Jewish people do not control General Motors or Ford Motor Co. The largest banks in this country have very few Jewish people on their boards of directors; the Jewish banks in New York have hardly more than 10 percent of all foreign loans. In the light of such facts, we can see that Jewish people are not generally the monied people.

Jewish people rose to the middle class by hard labor and application, long hours of work in the face of fierce competition. In these days of civil rights, we forget all too quickly the old quota system that was applied to Jewish students in our major universities, the severe restrictions in residential districts, and the many other forms of prejudice and hatred the Jews have encountered. All these served to make Jews more determined to succeed.

The belief that Jewish people are usually rich also permeates the scholarly world. In his essay "The Toynbee Heresy," Abba Eban quotes from Arnold Toynbee:

> "The Jews and the Pharisees are fossils of the Syriac society as it was before the Hellenic intrusion upon the Syriac world. . . . A number of fossils in Diaspora have preserved their identity through a devotion to religious rites and a proficiency in commerce and finance."

Eban replies to this assessment:

> The economic history of the Jewish people is in fact a poignant record with a ghastly volume of starvation and poverty. The legendary proficiency in commerce and finance is a characteristic which modern Israel has still failed to discover. But as for Dr. Toynbee it is sufficient to assert these time-worn platitudes.[1]

Too often Gentiles—Christians included—have perpetuated the fallacy by telling jokes concerning Jewish people and their money. On the other hand, we hear little about the many Jewish philanthropists who have given to worthy causes in their communities.

HE LOOKS LIKE A JEW

Some people claim they can recognize a Jew by his facial features, mannerisms, or speech. What they do not always take into account is that non-Jewish people can and sometimes do have the same characteristics.

Jewish people originated in the Mediterranean area. Their physical characteristics are often those of Mediterranean people. If Spaniards, Frenchmen, Italians, Greeks, Turks, Arabs, and Jews were mingling in one room, it could be difficult to pinpoint specifically Jewish features or mannerisms. Many Jewish people are fair-complexioned and have blond or red hair and blue eyes. If one, judging by "typical features," were to pick out the Jewish people

1. Abba Eban, *The Voice of Israel* (New York: Horizon, 1957), pp. 174-75.

from a variety of ethnic groups, he would very likely select most of the other Mediterranean persons as Jews before he chose any of the blond Jews. (Many western Christians can be cultural chauvinists when they consider other cultures and people to be inferior to their own. This is unfortunate inasmuch as the whole Body of Christ is an organic unity.)

Throughout the Western world, the Jews have assimilated much of the culture of the country in which they reside, and it is not always easy to distinguish the Jews from the other citizens of that country. American Jews are distinctly American, British Jews are distinctly British, and Russian Jews are distinctly Russian. More than 50 percent of the Jewish people have assimilated to the point where they have become a part of the culture.

We must see Jews as human beings who have every right to decency and dignity that anyone else has. We should treat them with respect and courtesy as we would like to be treated. Especially is this true if we want to reflect the life of Messiah within us. Knowing that He chose to be born to a Jewish family and live on earth as a Jew, we should do what He would have us do in our relations and attitudes to Jewish people.

THE CHARGE OF DEICIDE

Since Vatican II, many Roman Catholic and Protestant theologians have written volumes on the subject of deicide.[2] There seems to be some rethinking on the issue, but the full effect of the conclusions have yet to filter down to most of the nominal Christians in the pews, where some basic attitudes need to be changed.

Jews and Gentiles participated in the events at the end of Jesus' life. In Matthew 26:57-68 Jesus was tried by a Jew-

---

2. Deicide refers to the charge that Jewish people killed the Son of God; therefore, they have been called Christ killers. This charge had its origin in the third century (see chap. 2).

ish court. The Sanhedrin council did not accept the testi-
monies of the witnesses brought against Jesus; and if nothing more had been said, the trial would have come to an end
without a verdict. At the request for truth by the High
Priest, however, Jesus answered with the statement of His
identity (v. 64). The verdict of guilty was pronounced by
the High Priest on the basis of that single legal testimony
given under adjuration to speak the truth. Subsequently,
all of the Jewish people have been unjustly labeled Christ
killers down through the centuries.

What about the rest of the story? The Gentile side is
found in Mark 15:1-10. Pilate, the Roman governor, con-
demned Jesus, knowing that He was innocent: "Wishing to
satisfy the multitude, Pilate released Barabbas" (Mk 15:
15). Some say that Pilate would have released Jesus had it
not been for the howling mob. But this statement reflects
faulty reasoning on two accounts: (1) any judge who sur-
renders an innocent man to a howling mob is more guilty
than the mob, because he perverts his own chair of justice;
and (2) in that day only the Roman government had the
power to order execution. Pilate could have carried out
justice and saved an innocent man, but he did not. Luke
puts the scene into proper perspective: "For truly in this
city there were gathered together against Thy holy servant
Jesus, whom Thou didst anoint, both Herod and Pontius
Pilate, along with the Gentiles and the people of Israel"
(Ac 4:27). Both Jews and Gentiles were involved in the
action, and therefore it is not valid to blame only the Jews
for the crucifixion.

Also, not all Jewish people cried, "Let Him be crucified."
Did all Jews from Dan to Beersheba say it? Did Mary,
Simeon, Anna, or Mary Magdalene shout that? Remember
also that on the Day of Pentecost thousands of Jewish people and priests acknowledged their sins and became Messianic Jews. In time there were assemblies of Messianic

Jews all over the land (Gal 1:22). We must be careful to relate the full New Testament account from our pulpits. Sunday school lessons should be written authentically to present a true picture of first century Jewish life. Inaccurate, inflammatory accounts of the crucifixion have poisoned minds in every generation, shutting out the opportunity for meaningful sharing between Jews and Christians.

ATTITUDES

LOVE AND FRIENDLINESS

Love and friendliness must come first. The history of the Jewish people includes an appalling record of persecution by the Church. Not every Christian participated in this, however, and many groups have shown their love and concern for Jews. Through our words and actions we want to show our Jewish friends that Christians do love them. Really, of all people, Christians should be known as the best friends that Jewish people have.

NO ARGUMENTS

We should not argue when we share our faith. If we do, we may win the argument but lose the contact. We should not talk down to our Jewish friends but speak to them respectfully.

NATURALNESS

We need to be natural in faith sharing, but this is easier said than done. It is easy to talk about everyday matters; however, when we try to share our faith in the Messiah, we often freeze. We need to relax and converse well about a variety of subjects, yet be always alert for an opportunity to share our faith. We invite our Jewish friends to share their beliefs, and then we ask for an opportunity to express our beliefs. We trust the Spirit of God to do the rest.

EXPOSURE TO GOD

We want to expose our Jewish friends and ourselves to God Himself. Remember Israel's confession, Deuteronomy 6:4, "Hear, O Israel! The LORD is our God, the LORD is one!" Besides being a testimony to the unity of God, this is a command that we are to listen, to hear what God has to say to us. In exposing our Jewish friends to God, we must let the Word of God speak to us together.

TERMINOLOGY

If we want to communicate well, we must choose our words carefully. In faith sharing, it is important to use terms that will convey God's message clearly to the hearts of men. Through the centuries of Church history have arisen theological terms which Christians use in the Gentile world to communicate the Good News of salvation and to teach about the Christian life. For faith sharing with Jewish friends, we need to be selective in using communication which developed in the Gentile world, always keeping in mind the Jewish way of thinking and frame of reference.

Avoid pet phrases and traditional theological terms like *redemption, salvation,* and *being saved.* They may only create confusion; for instance, our Jewish friend, hearing the word *saved,* may think of being spared from injury in an auto accident or being rescued from drowning, while we have spiritual redemption in mind. Jews may use some of the theological words that we use, but they may attach different meanings to them.

SOME WORDS TO CONSIDER

CHRISTIANITY

The first word we want to clarify to our Jewish friends is *Christianity.* We should avoid using the term to mean "a religion better than the Jewish religion." Rather, in our faith sharing we want to emphasize that New Testament

Christianity is Jewish in its origin; it should not be regarded as foreign to Jewish people, because the New Testament builds on the Hebrew Scriptures. The New Testament teaches that Gentiles who come to the Messiah are spiritually related to Abraham through their faith. By no means is this Judaizing. Gentiles are not related to Abraham through acceptance of the terms of the Mosaic covenant; rather, they are related to him through their faith in Jesus as Messiah (Gal 3:29). By faith they partake of the life of the olive tree (Ro 11:17-18).

Barriers between the Church and the Jew developed because Gentile Christians in the third and fourth centuries were misrepresenting the message of the New Testament to the Jewish people. Those Christians forgot the solidarity between the Church and the Jews for two reasons: (1) they ignored Paul's teaching in Romans 11 that Christian beliefs are rooted in the Jewish "olive tree," and (2) the Church portrayed the Jews as a wicked people, causing a high wall of animosity to rise between them and itself.

In our faith sharing, we should point out that most first-century followers of Jesus the Messiah were Jewish. And, as Walter Wilson once said, a person who enters into the family of God is brought in by two Jews: Jesus and Paul. Most Christians in the first century were ethnically Jewish. The writers of the New Testament were Jews—with the exception of Luke, who may have been a Jewish proselyte. The rest of the writers are called by their Greek names, but we recognize their Aramaic or Hebrew equivalents: Peter—Simon (*Shim'on*) James—Jacob (*Ya'acov*), Jude—Judah (*Yehudah*), Paul—Saul (*Sha'ul*), and Matthew—Mattathiah (*Matai*), for examples.

Many of the first churches were founded and guided by Messianic Jews. Paul established churches throughout the Roman Empire. In the last chapters of many of his epistles, Paul refers to "my countrymen," and these were Messianic

Jews. Those zealous Messianic Jews of the first century represented the flower of the Jewish people as well as the early Church.

Therefore, when we tell our Jewish friends about Christianity, we should refer to it as the New Testament message proclaimed by Messianic Jews of the first century. In relating it to its first-century background, we show the real and original Christianity rather than the version produced in the fourth and fifth centuries. To communicate the Gospel message to Jewish people, we need to understand the first-century history and culture.

We should emphasize to our Jewish friends that it is *not* necessary that they repudiate their Jewish heritage if they come to believe in Jesus as the Messiah. We try to make our faith sharing as Jewish as possible without losing the biblical message. We want to help our Jewish friend understand that he need not say good-bye to his cultural background, sever himself completely from his national origin, and become something totally different: a non-Jew.

MESSIAH

We have already discussed the reason we use the term *Messiah* instead of *Christ*. We cannot charge anyone with rejecting Christ if he does not know who He is. And we do not tell our Jewish friends that they have rejected Christ when they do not know the biblical claims of the One they are reputed to have rejected. Did it ever occur to us that our Jewish friends may not have actually met the Messiah because they have not seen Him in the pages of the Hebrew Scriptures? Remember that Judaism includes the concept of the Messiah (see chap.8), and the Jewish person has his own concept of the Messiah. Thus, he may reject Jesus because He does not fulfill this traditional concept. We should emphasize and present the Messiah's ministry of humiliation and exchange-of-life principle. Our responsibility is to focus the attention of our Jewish friend on the

Scriptures. Then we must be patient, since comprehension of spiritual truth requires time.

ATONEMENT

Since the Jewish person probably would not understand our use of the word *salvation,* we build on the Jewish expression *atonement* in our faith sharing. According to the teachings of Judaism, atonement involves more than going to temple or synagogue on the Day of Atonement to pray and say certain prayers for the dead (although this day reminds him of these responsibilities). We have seen that in traditional Judaism atonement consists of the "great three" which Jewish leaders have substituted for the Temple sacrifices (see chap. 5).

One idea of the English word *atonement* is "at-one-ment" with God. Our sins are the great barrier between God and ourselves. Yet, when sins are cared for, it is possible for God to come near to us and to have fellowship with us, and for us to be at one with Him.

But the literal translation of the Hebrew word for *atonement* is "covering." *Day of Atonement* means "Day of Covering," or the day when sins are covered. God wants us to know there is a way to deal with sin. In the theocratic government the Mosaic constitution, there was a Day of Atonement. The Hebrew Scriptures speak of the covering for sin and the possibility of removing the sin barrier. Our Jewish friends can know this atonement, or salvation, in their lives, when we share the exchange-of-life principle.

REPENTANCE

Repentance, basically, is a turning. Judaism emphasizes turning from doing evil deeds to doing good deeds. Prayer also is emphasized. The "great-three" aspects are apparent: turning from doing evil deeds, performing good deeds, and praying. The Jewish person does all three to gain merit before God (see chap. 6).

Repentance is a good word to describe what everyone
needs to do when confronted with the truths of the Bible—
the Hebrew Scriptures and the New Testament. As we
share with our Jewish friends, we must emphasize that real
repentance means turning around to a right relationship
with God by turning around to face what the Scriptures say
about the Messiah and about our standing before God. We
must turn from our own works to acknowledge and receive
the Messiah and His work for our sins. Therefore, biblical
repentance is more than just turning from committing bad
deeds and doing some good deeds.

Repentance is a good New Testament word. Its New
Testament usage is based on the usage in the Hebrew Scriptures. The first Messianic Jewish preachers used the term.
Peter incorporated it in his message (Ac 2:38) : The people
had asked, "What shall we do?" and Peter said, "Repent,"
or, "Turn from the way you have considered Jesus of Nazareth and recognize Him and His Messianic claims."

Sin

In Judaism the concept of sin is usually associated with
social ills; it concerns how we treat our fellowman. Most
of Judaism's descriptions of sin refer to improper deeds or
motives in relating to others. Instructions are given in the
traditions regarding a proper behavior toward our fellow
human beings. Reform Judaism regards sin mainly as a
social evil and seeks to rectify the social and human ills of
the age.

We agree with these ideals, but we also go on to assert
that there is an even more basic implication in the biblical
concept of sin. We also affirm that there is a way we can be
freed from sin's shackles.

What do the Hebrew Scriptures say about sin? In faith
sharing, we look to God as He speaks to us through His
word. In Isaiah 53:6 we read, "All of us like sheep have
gone astray." This figure of speech refers to the well-known

behavior of sheep. If the lead sheep jumps in the wrong direction, the rest of the sheep will jump with him. It is the same with people; we are just like sheep who easily go astray. The verse continues: "each of us has turned to his own way." We all have our own ways of straying from right-eousness. Jeremiah described sin as God pictured it: "the heart is more deceitful than all else and desperately sick" (Jer 17:9). It is an unattractive description of man's plight, but this is what the Word of God says.

The Hebrew Scriptures speak of sin also in Psalm 51:5: "Behold, I was brought forth in iniquity, and in sin my mother conceived me." This passage teaches that the sin nature is transmitted from generation to generation. As we have already said, Orthodox and Conservative Jews do not accept the concept of original sin that each man inherits a sin nature which has been passed on from Adam (see chap. 5). They say that man must pull himself up by his boot-straps and realize his great potential. But this is what tradi-tion states, not what the Word of God says. We need to heed the biblical view of sin.

In Ezekiel we read, "The soul who sins will die" (Eze 18:4). Sin separates us from God; but through the ex-change-of-life principle, we receive a new nature, and our sins are taken away so that we can come into fellowship with God.

According to Psalm 103:12, our sins can be removed from us as far as the east is from the west. How do we measure the distance between east and west anywhere on our globe? In going north we can cross a certain point at the pole where we will begin to go south. But what point on the earth's surface do we cross where we are no longer going east but instead are going west? There is no such point. This is how far God says He wants to separate us from our sin; there will be no point of meeting—just as east never meets west. God's removal of sin is total.

As we share the Good News, there will come a time when

the Jewish person, if his heart is open, will long to be free from sin. But we must remember that it takes time to communicate the biblical view of sin. There must be both an intellectual understanding of the Scriptures and a work of the Spirit in the heart. We must patiently pray for the working of the Word through the activity of the Holy Spirit. A time will come when our Jewish friend will want to take the steps necessary for atonement.

CONVERSION

It is important to be aware that Jews and Christians attach different meaning to the term *conversion*. Evangelical Christians use it to mean the regeneration of the soul, that is, the experience of being born again. The Jewish person understands it to mean a distinct change of both religion and people. In the eyes of Jewish community, a Jew who converts becomes a Christian and is no longer Jewish. Unfortunately, this has long been the belief of the Church also.

But Jewish believers, or Messianic Jews, remain Jews ethnically; although spiritually they are part of the Body of the Messiah along with Gentile believers. (This will be discussed in chap. 10.) Our task in sharing our faith is not to rob the Jewish believer of his ethnic identity; rather, it is to help him realize that his soul will be enriched when he appropriates his kinship with other Messianic Jews.

Not all national Israel knew God or were obedient to His word, but in every generation in the days of the first and second Temples there were princes of faith, a remnant, who knew God and testified of His truths to their brethren. The Messianic Jew, while a part of the Body of Messiah in this age, also is in the line of those preceding princes of faith. When Messianic Jews share biblical truths to national Israel today, they function as those princes of faith.

Since *conversion* usually has a negative connotation to a Jewish person, it is best not to use the term. If we do use it, we must explain that Jews are not robbed of their identity if they become Messianic Jews. It is better to use the term *repentance* instead of *conversion,* since it is a term that Jewish people understand. In Hebrew Scriptures the word for *repentance* is sometimes translated "convert," for example, see Psalm 51:13. In our faith sharing we want to show that, when one does repent, he is regenerated—that is, experiences the new birth—and becomes a part of the Messiah's Body.

CONFESSION OF SIN

The expression *confession of sin* is likely to be misunderstood. A Jew may connect it with the Roman Catholic Confessional, and this is certainly not what we have in mind. Jewish tradition has an established procedure according to which a person is supposed to pray to God asking forgiveness for his sins, but this procedure is quite different from the biblical concept of confessing sins. We want to emphasize from Scripture the priority that confessing sin in regard to repentance involves the exchange-of-life principle. After atonement has been experienced, a biblical confession of sin involves one's daily walk with God.

9

SPECIFIC OBJECTIONS BY JEWISH PEOPLE

Through the years—due to cultural differences, misinformation, lack of information, and prejudice—Jews and Christians have held varying attitudes toward each other. Unfortunately, barriers have arisen between the two groups. The existence of these barriers is a tragedy because "mother-and-daughter" beliefs, Judaism and Christianity, should be able to exist side by side with mutual respect.

In this chapter, we shall treat some of the objections Christians may encounter when they witness to Jews. It is important to understand Jewish objections and listen sympathetically before we answer. We want a mutual rapport so both can share freely. As we share our beliefs, we trust the Holy Spirit to speak to hearts.

I HAVE MY OWN RELIGION; I DON'T WANT ANY OTHER RELIGION.

To this objection we reply that we certainly do respect an individual's religion. We desire to understand the various religions. We also desire to share our faith and trust in the Scriptures which were given to the Jewish people. It is these very Scriptures which teach us about God, our origin, and the sin that plagues the human race. These Scriptures also speak of a Messiah. They help us to recognize the Messiah and understand why He came to earth. The Word of God indicates that the descendants of Abraham are distinctive, and one Descendant is particularly distinctive. It is this One, the Messiah, who effects our atonement from sin[1] and gives assurance that we will enjoy eternal bliss with God. In other words, our faith is in the Jewish Messiah as a person spoken of in the Hebrew Scriptures, not in some kind of offshoot religion. It is not the merits of one religion over another that we share. Our personal relationship with this Messiah is what is so important: He said, "I am the way, and the truth, and the life; no one comes to the Father, but through Me" (Jn 14:6).

YOU TALK ABOUT THE FATHER, SON, AND HOLY SPIRIT: WE WORSHIP ONE GOD!

We need to make clear that we, too, are monotheists. We do not worship three gods!

There is a verse in the New Testament which says, "Great is the mystery of godliness" (1 Ti 3:16).[2] The nature of God is a mystery, and we are not able to fathom what He is. The Hebrew Scriptures state that no image should be made of God, and the implication is that it is impossible to understand God's essence. We are not to portray Him by material forms or by idols of mental concepts. However, that does not mean we cannot know anything about Him. What we can know is contained in His Word, which He was pleased to give through the Jewish people.

In answering the objection we build our case from Israel's great confession (Deu 6:4) as well as other passages from the Hebrew Scriptures; such as Genesis 1:26; Psalm 2:6-9; Proverbs 30:4; Isaiah 48:16—in addition to the revelation in the New Testament. The fuller discussion of the doctrine of God in chapter 5 should be examined thoroughly to help answer this objection.

---

1. It is here that we share the aspects of the exchange-of-life principle (see chap. 5).
2. Or the translation could be: "Great is the mystery of God!" His very nature is a mystery.

WE DON'T BELIEVE IN ORIGINAL SIN. HOW CAN WE, THOU-
SANDS OF YEARS AFTER ADAM, BE HELD RESPONSIBLE FOR
ADAM'S SIN?

To reply to this question, we should try to explain what
is meant by the term *original sin*. Because of Adam's transgression, the effect of disobedience is passed on to Adam's
descendants. That is, man today has a nature which is sinful and constantly prone to sin. The Jewish person miscon-
strues this to mean that man cannot help himself to do
anything good. Jewish thought wrestles with this idea because it seems unfair for two reasons: (1) man suffers because someone else disobeyed, and (2) man is hopelessly
bound to his nature.

According to his own concept of Adam's sin, the Jewish
person says that because of Adam's disobedience the sen-
tence of death is passed on to his progeny. We would agree
with this. The Jewish concept goes on to say it is entirely
possible for man to live an exemplary life and to make de-
cent, moral choices; by his own will man may rise to the
heights and show his great dignity because he is not com-
pelled to live on a low plane. We will also agree that a man
can lead a good life; he can live up to a beautiful ethic, raise
the level of society, and help his fellowman. However, a
man must face God, and it is God's declaration that all have
sinned and that we can never obtain His righteousness
through our own efforts.

One reason the Ten Commandments were given was to
reveal to man his real nature. In other words, the moral
law is like a mirror: when a man breaks commandments,
it shows him that he is a transgressor. But God was merci-
ful and provided a sacrificial system. The heart of this system is the sin offering. When one sinned in the days when
the Temple stood, the offerer could live, according to the
Mosaic covenant and on the basis of the life given by the
animal. This system showed that man could not satisfy
God's demand for righteousness through his own efforts.

According to the New Testament, the Messiah, as the perfect sacrifice, replaced the animals and gives His life to the one who believes in Him. So, while a man may do good in his relations with his fellowman, he can never have God's righteousness unless he has the life God wants to give him. To receive the life of the Messiah, the sinner must identify with the One who took his place and died for his sins, just as the Israelites of Temple days did with the animal. In answer to the Jewish objection, it is the exchange of life that releases a man from being bound to his sin nature.

Man is certainly in a state of sin. The Bible is replete with descriptions of this nature: our righteousnesses are as filthy rags (Is 64:6); each of us turns to his own way (Is 53:6); the heart is deceitful (Jer 17:9); we have all sinned (Ro 3:23). God's righteousness was never satisfied with a works righteousness. Note carefully the extended discussions in chapter 5 which deal with the doctrines of man, sin, and salvation.

OUR RABBIS TAUGHT US THAT REPENTANCE, PRAYERS, AND GOOD DEEDS ARE SUBSTITUTES FOR THE SACRIFICES; SO WHY TALK TO US OF SACRIFICES? BESIDES, THIS IS AN OLD-FASHIONED CONCEPT.

Again, the Word of God must be the final court of appeal. As we have seen, in the Mosaic covenant the sin offering dealt with the matter of sin; through this a man was to learn how to have a good standing in God's righteousness. In presenting the sin offering, a man had to repent of his sins and confess them. The offerer substituted the death of the animal in his place, and so he could go on living. The New Testament does not change this: we must repent, confess our sin, appropriate the Messiah's death for ourselves, and receive the very life of the Messiah.

Studying Jewish thought, we note that when the Temple was destroyed in 70 C.E., Jewish scholars substituted the formula of the great three for the sacrifices. Certainly there is nothing wrong with the spiritual exercises of repentance, prayer, and good deeds. These do demonstrate concern for oneself and society. However, they are substituted for satisfying God's righteousness, and this is contrary to what is taught by the sin offering of the Mosaic covenant and, for that matter, to the whole of Scripture. The Jewish scholars correctly point out that there was no opportunity to offer sacrifices after the Temple was destroyed, and so a *substitute* was needed. This is exactly the point. Note that the New Testament does not change the concept of the exchange-of-life principle! Again, as pointed out, no works righteousness can be substituted for the righteousness of God. God provided, in the work of the Messiah, a way by which we can satisfy His righteousness and He can give us the life of the Messiah as a new life.

WE BELIEVE IN TREATING PEOPLE WITH LOVE; WE WANT PEOPLE TO LIVE AT PEACE WITH ONE ANOTHER. WE DON'T WORRY ABOUT THE HEREAFTER!

We wholeheartedly agree that love is important! And this is the reason why we share mutual concerns with our Jewish friends: to indicate our love and concern. We indicate that we are vitally interested in them as a people, in their land, and in the problems they face. Of course, we know that most Jewish people have a concern for other people as well! We, too, are striving for a world of peace.

How are love and peace to be achieved? We feel that the Word of God explains why people cannot love as they ought and why they cannot do things they know they should do. The Bible speaks of man's sin nature and the sins people commit as a result of this nature. But when one receives God's righteousness, his entire nature is changed, and he can then have the best possible attitude toward his fellowman. In other words, God's righteousness enables one to demonstrate the most genuine care and concern.

Man is given a new dynamic of the power of God, which enables him to carry out the highest resolves and perform the greatest service for mankind.

Something more is involved, however. This encounter with the righteousness of God in the Messiah has eternal consequences; that is, it produces a relationship that lasts forever. *Only* the one who has the righteousness of God can enjoy the presence of God forever. No amount of works righteousness, as good as it may be, can give anyone the righteousness of God, according to His Word. If one has not received the righteousness of God, he can never enjoy the fellowship of God; when he dies he will be severed from God's presence. We need that encounter with the righteousness of God to safeguard our eternal destiny, as well as to receive the power by which to live the most useful lives here and now. All this is accomplished by what we call the exchange-of-life principle.[3]

YOU SAY MESSIAH HAS COME AND IS COMING AGAIN. WE BELIEVE HE IS STILL TO COME!

Here we are concerned with the identity of the Messiah. There were Jewish people in Jesus' day who did identify Jesus as the Messiah of Israel. Others did not. Where do we turn for answers? It must be to the Hebrew Scriptures, for here we find the description by which we can recognize the Messiah. The humiliation prophecies concerning the Messiah indicate where He was to be born, the manner of His birth, the reception given by His people, and the details of His death. But to this approach, the Jewish people will say that we are making the Scriptures fit our subject. Is this true? Suppose Jesus is not the Messiah. Then the Messiah to come will have to be someone just like Jesus, for Messiah must fulfill all these prophecies of humiliation. What is the

3. See chap. 6 in regard to the doctrine of salvation.
4. See chap. 8 for an extended discussion of the presentation of the Messiah.

possibility of the advent of another personality like Jesus? It is almost nil, from the human point of view.[4]

WHY DO CHRISTIANS HATE AND PERSECUTE THE JEWS?

Every genuine Christian feels grieved over the persecution which has been inflicted upon the Jewish people in the name of Christ and the cross. The result is that the message of the New Testament has been misrepresented and the Messiahship of Jesus has not been appreciated.[5]

This brings us to an important point. Jewish people must realize that not every Gentile is a Christian, not even all who attend a church regularly. It is entirely possible for a person to have a good intellectual knowledge of the facts of the New Testament and the ministry of Jesus of Nazareth and never experience that personal encounter with God by which he takes part in the exchange-of-life principle and possesses God's righteousness in the Messiah. That encounter is referred to as a spiritual rebirth, and it changes a person's entire nature, so that he becomes a new creation (2 Co 5:17). In the churches of Christendom are many people who have never experienced that spiritual rebirth. But Jewish people, as a rule, do not make distinctions like these; in their understanding, every church member is a Christian, no matter what his denomination or personal beliefs. In fact, Jewish people in the West are likely to believe that every Gentile is a Christian!

Obviously, this misunderstanding has its effects on the relationships between Jewish people and the Church. Church members who have never had a spiritual rebirth easily show displeasure with Jewish people. Hopefully, those who have had a genuine spiritual experience with the Jewish Messiah will show love and concern for Jewish people. Should it be otherwise?

5. See chap. 2 for a discussion of the relationship between the Jewish people and the Church.

I COULD'T BELIEVE IN JESUS; THAT WOULD MAKE ME A GEN-
TILE.

Many Jewish people feel strongly about their identity
and will not renounce it. Of course, when anyone acknowl-
edges and receives Jesus as Redeemer, he is not asked to renounce his identity. We point out that in 1 Corinthians
10:32 people are divided into three categories: Jews, Gentiles, and the Church of God (or Body of the Messiah).
The New Testament presents the picture that as the message of the Messiah is preached to all people (Jewish and
Gentile), some will respond, both Gentiles and Jews. Those
who respond become a part of the Body of the Messiah.

When a Swedish person responds, he becomes a part of
the Body of Messiah, but he does not cease to be Swedish.
Neither does a Jewish person cease to be a Jew. In the
Body of Messiah are Gentile Christians as well as Messianic
Jews. The Jewish person does not change his *ethnic* iden-
tity.

We base this assertion on a number of New Testament
passages as well as the composition of the early Church.
We have already pointed out that most of the original believers were Jewish. In no way did they seek to deny their
identity.

The New Testament itself never instructs Jewish believers to deny their Jewishness. Many Christians will emphasize that there is neither Jew nor Greek (Gentile) in
the Body of Christ; both are one, according to Galatians
3:28. However, what is the nature of this oneness? We
understand it to be spiritual. Jewish and Gentile believers
are one in the Spirit, and thus they are part of the one Body
of Christ. Galatians 3:28 also speaks of male and female,
and slaves and freemen. Although men and women, slaves
and freemen, are one as believers in the Messiah, they certainly do not shed their earthly distinctions. A man is a
man, and a woman is a woman, and unfortunately there are

servants of many kinds in this life. Therefore, while those in the Body of Messiah are one in the Spirit, earthly distinctions are not erased. And this applies to every ethnic group: a Jewish believer is Jewish, just as a Swedish believer is Swedish.

In the case of a Jewish inquirer, however, his national origin should be given attention because of the particular points of contact in faith sharing; such as, the Bible was written by Jews, and the Saviour is of Jewish extraction. Furthermore, it is extremely important that the Jewish believer retain his ethnic ties in the face of historical Church-Jewish antagonism. The Jewish believer must demonstrate his loyalty to his people so that he is not regarded as a traitor and stigmatized as anti-Jewish by his own people.

WHY DON'T OUR RABBIS UNDERSTAND AND ACCEPT WHAT YOU ARE TRYING TO SHARE WITH US?

Many rabbis do recognize the Gospels as fairly reliable in terms of history and geography. In fact, they may even admit Jesus is Messiah but not that He is divine, the true Messiah of Israel.

On the other hand, many rabbis and Jewish leaders have seen the Messiah of Israel in Jesus, or Yeshua. The disciples are one example. The New Testament indicated that a great company of priests were also obedient to the faith (Ac 6:7). Throughout the centuries, thousands of Jewish people have committed their faith to Jesus as Messiah and Redeemer.

We are also aware that many religious leaders in Christendom have not received the claims of Jesus as the Saviour. They have reservations concerning these claims and even deny many of them.

A person may be brilliant and highly educated, but he cannot know God solely through the intellect. True, the intellect is involved in an encounter with God in the Messiah. But it is also necessary to accept by faith the claims of the Messiah that He is the atonement for sin, that He is the only way to God, and that only in Him is there eternal and victorious life. Many religious leaders in the Church do not acknowledge this way of salvation.

Among Jewish scholars and religious leaders also, there are many who attempt to comprehend spiritual issues through the intellect alone. But intellect by itself is not able to grasp spiritual lessons; in fact, a strictly rational approach poses problems for talking in terms of biblical faith. Notice what Isaiah had to say when in his day it seemed that the messages of the prophets were not received (Is 29:10-12). When the message was delivered to one who was learned, he answered that the message was closed; and when the message was given to one who was not learned, he replied that he was not learned. Neither the learned nor the unlearned can grasp through a rational approach the spiritual import of the Word.

We may say, in love and compassion, that this might very well be the case today. Do our Jewish friends spiritually perceive the message of the Word of God? How do the learned and the unlearned come to the Bible? The Word gives us the answers for this life and declares to us the way to the presence of God after this life. All of us must grasp the Word intellectually and respond by faith to what it says.

WE JEWISH PEOPLE ARE NOT DIFFERENT FROM OTHERS. WHY CAN'T YOU JUST LET US LIVE OUR OWN LIVES? WE DO NOT BOTHER OTHERS.

This is not easily answered. There was a time when Jewish people were isolated in ghettos, and many did not have the opportunity to mix with society in general. Obviously, the ghetto was not the solution, but this objection expresses a ghetto aloofness. Ignoring people is not the approach to any kind of human relationship; it would not be long before the Jewish person would be wondering why people were ignoring him!

The fact of the matter is that the Jewish people cannot just evaporate. They are not different on the human level, yet the Bible puts the Jewish people right in the center of the platform of world history. The Abrahamic covenant guarantees that the Jewish people will exist as long as human history continues (Gen 17:7). The Bible indicates that the Messiah came from the Jewish people; Jesus Himself said that salvation is of the Jews (Jn 4:22). The Word of God prophesies that through the Jewish people blessings are going to come upon the world when the Messiah rules over it. From God's point of view, the Jewish people are different. Try as hard as they may, the Jewish people never will be able to completely assimilate with other peoples, because God has a purpose for them.

To be utterly fair in our faith sharing, we have to go to all people. To exclude Jewish people would be the height of discrimination. When we share with Jewish people as well as with all others, we show our Jewish neighbors that they are not left out of the interest of those who believe in Jesus the Messiah.

I don't believe in the Bible anymore; it's full of mistakes. Science has all the answers.

This attitude is very prevalent today, as people question the authority of the Scriptures. Many trust science, since the technological developments of the past few years have revolutionized our entire society. They feel that the Bible is outmoded and does not have the answers for today's questions.

We do not disparage scientific achievement. Our standard of living is higher than our forefathers could have dreamed because of technological advancements. The scientific method is an excellent tool for the area in which it operates.

But does this solve all the problems we face today? Does a bigger and faster jet assuage fear and minimize prejudice?

Does a satellite communication system raise the moral level of our youth? Does nuclear fission control men's hearts to restrain aggression (other than through fear of retaliation)? While the scientific method does wonders in the area of technology, moral and spiritual areas of life are not improved by a purely materialistic approach to solving our problems.

A number of disciplines have served to establish the accuracy of the historical and geographical statements in the Word of God. Archaeology has done much in the last several decades to support the historical narratives and show that the biblical record is correct historically, geographically, and culturally.

True, there are many questions regarding creation, that is, the how of things. But this does not mean that the Scriptures cannot have a message in this area; they do, if properly understood. The Bible emphasizes what did take place. The Bible also states many of God's purposes and gives the why to the basic problems of man, and it gives answers also. We recommend studying the Scriptures for a sound evaluation. It always has a message if one will listen: "Hear, O Israel!" (Deu 6:4).

FOR FURTHER STUDY

Many groups, including Christian service organizations, that relate to Jewish people have literature which will supplement chapter 10, as well as discuss other subjects that help in faith sharing. These groups will be only too glad to send their literature to you, usually for a free-will offering.

10

MESSIANIC JUDAISM AND ITS CONTRIBUTIONS

A Plea for Faith Sharing

The pages of one chapter could not contain a fraction of the long list of Jewish people who have turned to Jesus as the Messiah, much less include a description of their many contributions. The Jewish people who have responded to this message have provided much to the ongoing of the Church.

Too Few Returns for the Investment?

The attitude of many Gentile Christians toward sharing their faith with Jewish people is exemplified in an experience I had. A pastor and I were discussing the challenge of missions around the world. When the discussion turned to sharing the Messiah with Jewish people, the pastor became quite nervous and mumbled something about "very poor returns" for all the effort and money expended. He went on to say that a well-known evangelist had won hundreds of people to Christ during the year, but only fourteen of them were Jewish. Therefore, the pastor concluded, the church should not invest in a field which yielded so few returns.[1] This attitude is prevalent among many Gentile Christians, among pastors as well as lay people.

1. This attitude is frequently encountered. It is reflected in missionary budgets which do not allow a cent for work among Jews, in spite of the fact that Gentile Christians have a rich heritage from Jewish people in the very Bibles they read, as well as in the Saviour whom they adore. It is also reflected in missionary conferences which do not include a speaker to talk on behalf of faith sharing with Jewish people.

What Do the Scriptures Say?

We must heed what Paul wrote in his letter to the Romans: "Now if their transgression be riches for the world and their failure be riches for the Gentiles, how much more will their fulfillment be!" (Ro 11:12). Many Bible scholars interpret this passage to mean that at the end of this age Jewish people will have their fulfillment when many of them will be restored to favor and fellowship with God. However, we ought to take a second look at the verse. Why must we wait until the distant future? Why can't this begin to take place now? Certainly when Jewish people turn to Jesus the Messiah, their fulfillment is of great value. Not only is their fellowship with God of great personal value to them, but there is also a great contribution to the Church in this age.

The Church has received specific instructions concerning its responsibility to share its faith. Paul says in Romans that, as we share about our peace of heart, assurance of eternal life, and knowledge of sins atoned—all of which are achieved through a godly life—our Jewish friends will desire what we have (Ro 11:11, 14).[2] Of course, this approach prompts us to search our hearts to see if we actually speak and live in such a way that our Jewish friends will want Jesus the Messiah.

These passages emphasize the Church's responsibility to Jewish people. At the very heart of Church-Jewish relationships must be respect for each other's beliefs. We are to respect the religion which Jewish people practice, and we must never forget that this religion is based on biblical revelation and the traditions. On the other hand, Jewish people are to respect genuine Christians who seek to live according to both the Hebrew Scriptures and the New Testament. Part of New Testament practice is faith sharing, as we have already seen; therefore, we should not be asked

2. It has been put this way: "We are to make their mouths water for what we have!"

to forego this merely to be agreeable to people. There are many within Christendom who, having minimized the main biblical doctrines anyway, insist that the Church and Jewish people present their religions on a social basis alone. However, when each is true to himself and honest with the other, there can be opportunity to share our faith in a context of mutual love and compassion. Faith sharing must be done without sacrificing biblical principles and the biblical doctrines upon which they are based.

THE RESPONSE

The response of Jewish people to the biblical message is much greater than most people think. On a percentage basis, more Jewish people respond to the message of Jesus the Messiah than do Gentile people. This is almost unbelievable. However, if we take the figure of the Jewish people who acknowledged Jesus as the Messiah in the last century— 224,000 of 18 million Jewish people—this amounts to about 1.2 percent.[3] Already in the first half of this century, the 224,000 figure has been exceeded; and if present trends continue through the second half of the twentieth century, the figures for the first part will be exceeded. However, we will take just the nineteenth-century figures. If 1.2 percent of all Gentiles living in the nineteenth century had come to the Messiah, that would have resulted in a total of 24 million believers (based on a 2 billion population).

IN THE EARLY CHURCH

Material concerning Messianic Jewish people and their contributions is difficult to find in the ancient world once we get beyond the first century and the New Testament. One ancient source which covers the first century and the

3. These figures were estimated by Pastor de le Roi in his *Juden Mision, a History of Protestant Missions Among the Jews Since the Reformation,* as cited by A. Bernstein, *Some Jewish Witnesses for Christ* (London: Operative Jewish Converts' Inst., 1909), p. 10.

first part of the second century is Hegesippus. According to Eusebius, Hegesippus was a Messianic Jew in the land of Israel and in later life lived in Rome about 150 c.e. Hegesippus supplies information about various Jewish sects which gives us clues about Jewish people who acknowledged Jesus. Fragments of his work have been preserved in Eusebius's *History IV*. The early Church was mainly Jewish, and we have seen how gloriously those Messianic Jews carried their faith across the Roman world.

Of interest is the list of Messianic Jews who pastored the church at Jerusalem. We know from the New Testament (Gal 1:19) that James held the position of leading elder in the Jerusalem church. Hegesippus states in his writings that James was martyred in the Temple around 62 c.e. The succession of Messianic Jewish leaders was Symeon in 62 c.e., Justin I in 64, Zacheus in 112, Tobias in 114, Benjamin in 116, Justin in 118, Matthais in 120, Phillip in 122, Seneca in 125, Justus II in 126, Levi in 128, Ephres in 130, Joseph in 132, and Jude in 133. It is readily apparent that each man's term of leadership was very brief. One reason probably was the intense persecution which the leaders experienced.

The Talmud supplies information concerning Jewish believers, who were regarded as apostates at the time of the early Church. If nothing was ever said, we would wonder about the presence and activity of Messianic Jewish people. This reaction by Jewish rabbis can only indicate the presence of many Jewish believers who had a very active and vital ministry.

A number of passages in the Talmud demonstrate that Jewish leaders were acquainted with the New Testament. In one case, a rabbi quoted from Matthew 5:17, altering it slightly to suit his own purposes, when someone asked him to settle a legal dispute. "I have not come to destroy the law of Moses, nor have I come to add to the law of Moses"

(Shabbat 116*b*). Rabbinical knowledge of the New Testament is seen also in the dialogue with Rabbi Trypho and Justin Martyr. These and numerous other instances show that many Jewish leaders were acquainted with the New Testament and that there were many Jewish believers.

Historical evidence indicates that there were Jewish believers in both the eastern and the western churches in the period of the Gᵉmara (200-500) and in the Middle Ages. We have seen what happened between the Church and Jewish people. That some Jews became believers in spite of all that occurred can be attributed only to the mercy and grace of God. God will have His way in spite of hindrances produced by men, but woe to those responsible for the hindrances (Mt 18:7). The Messianic Jews in these periods contributed greatly to various studies of the Word of God for the glory of the Messiah.

We come to the modern period, the 1800s and 1900s. Pastor de le Roi, a Jewish missionary historian, is remembered for his collection of statistics pertaining to Jewish believers of the various churches. It was his opinion that in the nineteenth century the number was as high as 224,000. In addition to determining the number of Jewish believers, he has also given us a large collection of biographical sketches.[4] As W. T. Gidney of the London Society has observed, "Jewish believers were to be *weighed* as well as counted."[5]

SOME MESSIANIC JEWS

In this section we will discuss a few of the more outstanding Messianic Jews and their contributions. Their life stories are simply amazing. Remember that in each case a believer took the opportunity to share his faith with the Jewish person. We can see God's blessing on the effort.

4. Bernstein, p. 10.
5. Ibid.

MICHAEL SOLOMON ALEXANDER: BISHOP OF JERUSALEM

Michael Alexander was the first Protestant bishop of Jerusalem in modern times. He ministered in the mid-nineteenth century, about thirty years before the initial emigration of Jews to the land of Israel laid the foundations for modern Israel. It could very well be said that God planted this man in Palestine to be a testimony in the midst of those strategic events.

Michael Alexander was born of Jewish parents in Posen, Prussia, in 1799. He was reared in the strict manner of Rabbinical Judaism. When he was sixteen years old, he had the distinction of being a teacher of Talmud as well as of the German language. When he was twenty-one years old, he went to England to continue his teaching career as well as to perform the duties of a *shoḥet* (ritual slaughterer).

At this time he knew nothing of the existence of the New Testament. But when he moved to Colchester, he noticed a handbill describing a meeting of the London Jews' Society. His curiosity was aroused, and he purchased a New Testament and began to read it secretly. Meanwhile he became a rabbi at Norwich.

Rev. B. B. Golding of the Plymouth parish came to him for lessons in Hebrew; and from time to time, between sessions of Hebrew language study, the two discussed Jesus. Alexander experienced great inner conflict; and, the story goes, on Sunday evenings he would stand in the shadows of the Stonehouse Church and listen to the music.

Because of his increasing interest in the New Testament, he was suspended from his post as rabbi. Subsequently he began attending the Stonehouse Church. Shortly thereafter he and his wife became believers. As Alexander had an excellent grasp of the Word, he soon became involved in various teaching ministries. In 1827 he was ordained. As a member of the London Jews' Society he served as a missionary in Danzig from 1827 to 1830 and then in London from 1830 to 1841. While in London he often preached to Jewish people and also took an active part in revising the Hebrew New Testament and translating the Anglican Liturgy into the Hebrew language.

In 1841 Michael Alexander was consecrated as a bishop by the Archbishop of Canterbury, and in the same year he went to Israel as the first Protestant bishop of Jerusalem. He served there only four years; however, in those four years the Lord used him in a very wonderful way. At the end of only one year of work he wrote, "We have had every ordinance of our church performed in our chapel." He died in Egypt but was buried in Jerusalem in the English cemetery. A crowning testimony to his ministry was a letter signed by thirty-one Jewish believers in Jerusalem, paying eloquent tribute to his service for the Lord.

DAVID BARON: WRITER AND WITNESS TO HIS OWN PEOPLE

David Baron labored for many years with the Mildmay Mission in London. Later he founded the Hebrew Christian Testimony for Israel. He was born and reared in Russia in a traditional Jewish home and was an exceptionally gifted child. It is said that at four-and-a-half years of age he could read Hebrew fluently. The boy experienced several misfortunes, including suffering from a serious illness and later being injured by a horse. In experiencing these mishaps, he displayed a keen sense of the presence of God. When he was ten years old, he entered a school for rabbinical studies and excelled in his studies. When he became Bar-Miṣvah, he delivered a speech entitled "The Necessity of Putting Away Leaven." Everyone realized that this boy had a piety and a learning that were well beyond his years.

Due to a number of circumstances, David Baron traveled to England, arriving there without any friends or means of support. He was befriended by Koenig, a Messianic Jewish man who worked with the Mildmay Mission. David regarded Christians as idolators, but Koenig continued to show him love and concern. David felt obliged to reciprocate Koenig's benevolence, and he attended the meetings conducted by Koenig. After attending several and meeting many of the Jewish believers of the Mildmay Mission, he went through a period of spiritual distress as he struggled with the truths of the New Testament. His friends reminded him that the only way to end the struggle was to trust Jesus the Messiah as his Saviour. Finally he knelt and called on God to save him in the name which he had despised for so long. When he arose from his knees, he felt a great peace in his soul. The Scriptures, especially the Psalms, assumed a new, personal meaning for him. In October 1878 he publicly confessed his faith in Jesus the Messiah.

After a period of training David Baron began to work with the Mildmay Mission. He traveled extensively throughout the British Isles and Europe, and in 1890 he was sent to eastern Europe. From there he went to Jaffa, Israel, to preach the Messiah to the Jewish immigrants who were coming into the country.

With the help of friends David Baron established a center for a new work, The Hebrew Christian Testimony to Israel, in London. He also produced a large volume of writings. He continued to travel widely in Europe and was invited to the United States several times by D. L. Moody to speak at the Northfield Convention. He died in 1926, but the work which he founded continues to this day. Many of David Baron's friends testified that he was the most Christlike man they had ever known.

Paul Cassel: Theologian

Paul Cassel was one of the most eminent theologians of

the German Reformed church. He had such a reputation that Jewish people themselves said, "A Jew like Cassel is an honor to his former brethren in the faith."

He was born in Silesia in 1821. At the University of Berlin he distinguished himself in his studies in history and theology, and became a philologist, with a knowledge of Latin, Greek, and other languages. He worked for a time as a journalist.

While working as a journalist, he began to amplify a systematic study of Israel's history. This necessitated that he read the New Testament in order to understand why there was a barrier between the Church and the Jewish people. In reading the New Testament he became convinced that Jesus' claims to be the Messiah were true. Also he had the fellowship of a number of Gentile Christians who were a great blessing to him. In 1855 he confessed his faith in Jesus the Messiah.

His accomplishments brought him many honors, especially in the fields of history and theology. In 1859 he began to preach in Berlin and drew great crowds of Jewish and Gentile people. This gave him further distinction throughout Germany.

In 1868 he joined the staff of the London Jews' society and, as pastor of Christ Church, carried on a pulpit ministry for twenty-three years, drawing large congregations week in and week out. Usually many Jewish people were in attendance at the meetings. What brought him recognition in the Jewish community was his consistent and effective reputation of being against all the anti-Semites. The Jewish people said of him, "Though he has left us, he is by no means our enemy." It is estimated that 260 Jewish people confessed Jesus as Messiah during his ministry.

Paul Cassel was a prolific writer and published many scholarly works, some of which have been translated into English. He died in 1893, just before Christmas.

ALFRED EDERSHEIM: SCHOLAR, PREACHER, AND PASTOR

Alfred Edersheim is well known by ministers and educators for his work *The Life and Times of Jesus the Messiah.* He was born in Vienna in 1825 of well-to-do parents. He was a student at the University of Budapest and on the way to becoming a great scholar. He spoke Latin fluently and knew Greek, German, French, Hebrew, Hungarian, and Italian. While at the University of Budapest, Edersheim was introduced to a number of Christian ministers, one of whom was the well-known Dr. Duncan, missionary of the Church of Scotland in Hungary. Dr. Duncan was a well-educated man who also spoke Latin fluently. This skill attracted Edersheim to him, and over the years a strong bond of friendship grew between them.

After Duncan left Hungary, a Gentile Christian minister became Edersheim's tutor in English. Because of the minister's prayers and faith sharing, it was not long before the young student recognized Jesus as the Messiah and confessed Him as His Saviour. Edersheim then went to Edinburgh, where he completed his training in theology. He was ordained by the Church of Scotland and sent to Rumania as a missionary. After many trials and tests there, he finally settled down in England and was also ordained by the Church of England.

Edersheim, a great preacher, was the first Messianic Jew invited to preach in Westminster Abbey. He served for a time as the preacher at the University of Oxford, and in 1883 he became a lecturer at Oxford. This provided him the opportunity to write several works, including *The Life and Times of Jesus the Messiah,* which only a Messianic Jew could have produced. Toward the end of his life, he moved to southern France, where he died in 1889.

SOLOMON GINSBURG: MISSIONARY

An amazing story of faith is the life of Solomon Ginsburg,

a Messianic Jew who opened up the Amazon Valley to the preaching of the Good News of salvation. He was born in a strict Orthodox family in Poland. At six years of age he was sent to relatives in Königsberg, Germany, to obtain a better education. When he was fourteen, he returned home and found that he was in conflict with traditional Judaism. On the following observance of the Feast of Tabernacles, while listening to the religious discussion, he casually picked up the book of Isaiah and opened it to chapter 53. He asked his father to whom the prophet was referring, and his father was startled by the question. The boy repeated it, but his father did not answer and snatched the book away.

When Solomon learned shortly afterward that a bride had been chosen for him, he ran away from home. He traveled to London, where he worked for a relative. Someone invited him to a service at the Mildmay Mission to hear an explanation of Isaiah 53—a providential circumstance in light of what had happened in his family's private booth at the Feast of Tabernacles. Solomon was impressed by the message, and he obtained a copy of the New Testament. It was through the reading of the New Testament that he received Jesus as his Messiah and Saviour. His family attempted to change his mind but failed, and Solomon left the home of his relatives. A number of other relatives came to England to reason with him about the "error of his ways," but Solomon's mind was made up; but he remained in contact with his family.

He prepared for the ministry and felt called to go to Brazil as a missionary. Solomon's missionary work led him into the jungles where his life was often in danger. On one occasion when he was threatened by brigands, one of the desperadoes sought him out, and Solomon fully expected to die at his hands. Much to his surprise, the man did not kill him but said instead that he would not harm such a good man. He had sensed the love and concern in the heart of this Messianic Jew. In time, Solomon was able to lead many of these desperadoes to the Lord.

Following the example of Paul, he traveled from place to place. As he preached, he formed his new believers into local assemblies and selected elders to handle the preaching and teaching. In this way he established many churches in various parts of Brazil.

Solomon had training in printing, and he began publishing papers and booklets. Soon a stream of his literature was flowing into all parts of Brazil. Many people came to know of him and affectionately called him Pastor Ginsburg. He died in 1927.

ISAAC LICHTENSTEIN: RABBI WHO PREACHED JESUS

This man has one of the most amazing stories of the nineteenth century. He was born in the early 1800s and was a rabbi before he was twenty. For several years he had an itinerant ministry in Northern Hungary but finally became a district rabbi in a town called Tapio Szele, where he served for almost forty years.

One day, early during his rabbinate, he found a New Testament in one of his district schools. He became agitated with its presence, and he took it home and in extreme anger threw it onto one of the shelves in his own library. He forgot about it, and there it lay untouched.

After thirty years went by, there was an anti-Jewish drive in Hungary, and Rabbi Lichtenstein was puzzled. He wondered what prompted so-called Christian enmity against the Jews and wanted to make a study of it. In the process of his research, he came across the New Testament in his library and began to read it very carefully. As he did so, he was convinced more and more that Jesus is the Messiah, and a strange feeling began to awaken in his own heart. He later expressed his convictions in one of his publications: "The half has not been told to me of the greatness and power and glory of this Book which was sealed at one time to me. It all seemed so new, and yet it did me so much good." He compared the New Testament to a bride dressed in wedding clothes and adorned with jewels.

He said nothing of his convictions for three years, then he began to use material from the New Testament in his preaching. This, of course, intrigued and astonished his listeners. One Saturday morning in his message he openly admitted that he took his material from the New Testament. Then he spoke of his belief that Jesus is the Messiah and Redeemer of Israel.

In rapid order he published three pamphlets telling of his belief. Jewish people in Hungary and throughout central Europe were amazed that this old and respected rabbi still in office was calling upon his people to acknowledge Jesus as the Messiah.

Of course, as soon as other rabbis realized what was taking place, he was called before the chief rabbi in Budapest and asked to recant his beliefs. Lichtenstein said that he would do so only if they could prove him wrong. The chief rabbi proposed that he believe whatever he wanted but not preach Jesus the Messiah publicly. The pamphlets which he had written would be counteracted by an official statement by the chief rabbi. Lichtenstein replied that he was in his right mind and would not recant. At that, the Jewish leaders asked that he resign his position and be baptized. He declared that he had no intention of being formally baptized or joining any church since he wanted to remain with his congregation.

Strangely, he was able to remain with his congregation, although he suffered much because of his beliefs. His congregation also felt the pressure, but they staunchly supported their rabbi. Lichtenstein continued to teach and preach, using the New Testament. This unusual situation attracted attention from all over Europe, especially from various missionary societies as well as the Roman Catholic authorities. He received many tempting offers to be either a missionary or a pastor, but he answered that he felt he should remain among Jewish people and be as Jeremiah was among his people—a watchman upon the walls to plead the case for Jesus the Messiah.

Finally he did resign his office as district rabbi and settled in Budapest, where he carried on a writing ministry. For over twenty years he traveled to all parts of the continent with the truth as he saw it in Jesus. His plea was always as it comes in Hosea 14:1: "Return, O Israel, to the LORD your God." By now he was an elderly man, beloved by many Jewish people and Christians alike, though of course disliked by many of the Jewish leaders. His entrance into the presence of the Lord in 1909 was a triumphant one, as he testified to the one Messiah, Jesus, who gave His life for the salvation of men.

ISIDOR LOWENTHAL: TRANSLATOR OF THE AFGHAN BIBLE

Isidor Lowenthal was thirty-eight years old when he was gunned down in India. But his brief life was given over to the Messiah and had tremendous consequences for India and Afghanistan.

He was born in Poznan, Poland, to an orthodox Jewish home. He graduated from the gymnasium (preparatory school for the university) where he had been an excellent student. His father wanted him to pursue a business career, but Lowenthal had no taste for it. A short while later he emigrated to the United States, thinking he would find employment there. Although he was educated, this immigrant could not find work and finally became a peddler. In Wilmington, Delaware, on a cold, rainy night in November, he sold some of his wares to a pastor. The pastor noticed his plight and invited him to spend the night in his home. In conversation that evening, the pastor learned that his guest was an accomplished linguist with an extraordinary education. The pastor obtained for him a position as a teacher of German and French in a college in Pennsylvania.

The worshipful atmosphere in the pastor's home had impressed Lowenthal, and he began to attend services in the pastor's church. This led him to study the Scriptures, and finally he was convinced that Jesus was the Messiah. It was no easy decision to make. During the struggle before he made his decision, a young Messianic Jew, a roommate of Lowenthal at the college where he taught, had shared his faith with him. What Lowenthal had seen in the pastor was also evident in the heart and life of his young Messianic Jewish roommate. Eventually, Lowenthal made a public confession of his faith in Jesus and joined the church where his pastor friend was the minister.

He continued to teach until he entered Princeton Theological Seminary in 1852. He graduated with the highest of honors and was a speaker at his graduation ceremony, his address concerning missions in India. After graduation he offered himself as a missionary to India and was sent by the board of foreign missions.

When he arrived in India, he began to study the languages: Hindustani, Persian, and Pushtu (the language commonly used in Afghanistan). Lowenthal also mastered Arabic so he could discuss his faith with Muslims. Because of his great gift as a philologist, he was able to master these languages within a year.

Later he was sent to a town located on the border between India and Afghanistan to wait for an opportunity to enter Afghanistan. While waiting, he continued his study of the Pushtu language and began translating the New Testament into this language. He had no access to any grammar or dictionary, but this able linguist set out on his task. He checked his translation of the New Testament with both the most learned people and the people on the street. People loved Lowenthal and listened to him intently. Even the fanatical Muslim listened to what this man had to say.

In 1864, just when it seemed that the way would be opened for him to enter Afghanistan, he was accidentally shot by one of his own servants. His death seemed a tragedy, but with God there are no mistakes. On Lowenthal's desk were his gifts to Afghanistan: the New Testament in Pushtu, the nearly completed Pushtu dictionary, and other materials he had written.

Samuel Zwemer said that, among the heroes of missions in Islam, foremost is Isidor Lowenthal, the ambassador of Jesus the Messiah to the remote country of Afghanistan.

Auguste Neander: Scholar and Father of Modern Church History

He was born David Mendel and was destined to become the father of modern church history. This Messianic Jew was to become a prominent figure in the universities of Germany. He was born in Germany in 1789 and was a descendant of the reformer of traditional Judaism, Moses Mendelsohn. Neander received his early education in Hamburg and was influenced by classmates to examine the claims of Jesus the Messiah. When he did, he acknowledged Jesus as Messiah. Upon formally acknowledging his faith he took the name Neander. (The Church's practice then was to have Jewish believers change their names.)

He studied at the University of Halle under the father of theological modernism, Schleiermacher. Neander was able to absorb Schleiermacher's theology, but it did not deter Neander's own theological stand. In later years, while Schleiermacher was teaching at the University of Halle at one end of the hall, Neander lectured from time to time at the other end of the hall. While Schleiermacher is regarded as the father of modernism, it was Neander who held the day for evangelicalism in Germany.

After leaving Halle, Neander continued his theological studies and became well known as a historian. He eventually had a position as professor in the University of Berlin and was known as one of the leading lecturers at the university until the day he died. Many people, Protestants and Roman Catholics alike, came to hear his lectures.

Neander had a disposition that attracted people to his Messiah. The students regarded him as a father and counselor. He was a tremendously prolific writer. Never having married, he was able to devote all of his time to his studies and writing.

The supreme object of Neander's life and labors was to tell the story of the Church of Christ, and he produced a work that earned him the title of champion for evangelicalism in Germany. In writing his *Life of Christ,* he set out to counteract the theology of Schleiermacher. In this work, he demonstrated the validity of the scriptural record in an attempt to stem the tide of higher criticism. He had many other works to his credit, which have been translated into English. Some of them are *The History of the Planting and Training of the Christian Church by the Apostles* and biographies of Julian the Apostate, Bernard, and Chrysostom. An unfinished work, which has not been translated into English, is his *Life of the Apostle Paul.* It is said that he died while dictating a page of his *General History,* which had to be completed from his notes after his death. As he died, he said, "I am weary; I must sleep. Good night."

What a story this is! Because some students took the time to share the Messiah with this man, he became greatly influential in the schools of learning in Germany to the honor and glory of Jesus the Messiah.

SAMUEL ISAAC SCHERESCHEWSKI: BISHOP IN CHINA AND BIBLE TRANSLATOR

The story of Schereschewski leads us to China, where he served the Lord for many years. He was born in Russian

Lithuania in 1831. His early training was in traditional Judaism, and from the beginning he showed an aptitude for languages. Eventually he became a student at the University of Breslau, and he seemed destined to be a scholar of the Talmud. However, in retrospect we know that God had a special work for Him.

The London Missionary Society was, in his student days, producing a Hebrew translation of the New Testament. A copy of the translation fell into the hands of Schereschewski, and he read it avidly. As he read, he became convinced that Jesus is the Messiah.

However, for Schereschewski to follow Jesus as his Messiah and Saviour in an extremely Orthodox section of Europe would have created a scandal. Therefore, after confessing his faith he emigrated to the United States. In 1857 he entered the theological seminary in New York to learn Koine[6] Greek of the New Testament.

Schereschewski was puzzled by the great number of Protestant denominations but finally joined the Episcopal church. He then accompanied another Episcopal bishop to China, and it seemed that this was the Lord's place for him. Before long, he realized that his special work was in the area of translation. He grasped the Chinese language rapidly, and within a year he began to translate the prayer book into Mandarin. In 1865, as one of a committee of five Chinese and five English-speaking scholars, Schereschewski began to translate the New Testament into the Mandarin dialect. After this was completed in 1865, Schereschewski, by himself, began to translate the Old Testament into Mandarin. His translation was completed in eight years. Schereschewski's contribution in the missionary effort in China was to give the Bible to the people in their own language.

6. The street-language Greek of Paul's day, in which the New Testament was written.

In 1875 he was elected bishop of Shanghai. He initially refused the position but accepted it two years later. He then began to translate the prayer book into the Wen-li dialect, which was the Chinese classic style. In 1881 he was struck with paralysis. He resigned as bishop, since he felt that it was not right to retain the office while he was ill. Many people might discontinue their work in the face of ill health, but not Schereschewski. His mind was keen; and therefore he felt that, as long as he had some strength, he would continue to translate the Word of God into the language of the Chinese people. There were few men as well qualified for the task. Max Mueller, one of the great philologists of Oxford University, classified Schereschewski as one of the six most learned Orientalists in the world in the nineteenth century.

Eventually Schereschewski became so incapacitated that he could not even hold a pen. However, he was able to type with his index fingers and so produced a revised translation of the Old Testament in Mandarin.

But this was not the end of his labors. He worked for another score of years in various parts of the Orient, including Japan, wherever he could be near a printing press which he could use. Just before his death he completed the translation of the entire Bible, including the Apocrypha, into the Wen-li dialect.

He died in Tokyo in 1906, four years after the publication of his Bible. His life is another brilliant chapter in the annals of Messianic Judaism.

JOSEPH WOLFF: DAVID LIVINGSTONE TO THE JEWISH PEOPLE

The work of Joseph Wolff has been compared to that of David Livingstone. While Livingstone opened up the African continent to the Good News of salvation, Joseph Wolff sought out the Jewish people scattered throughout North Africa and Asia.

He was born in Bavaria around 1795. His father was a rabbi to a small group of Jewish families. Soon after Joseph was born, the family moved to Halle. In his early years, Wolff received a strict Jewish education. He was then sent to a Christian school, but only to learn the German language. At eleven years of age he was placed in a Protestant school but was dissatisfied with it. Soon after, he entered a Roman Catholic school, and there he learned about Frances Xavier, who became a hero to him. He made up his mind to become a believer in order to be a missionary like Xavier. He still was not sure of his faith, and he wandered in various places. Eventually he arrived at Prague, and there he did confess his faith in Jesus as the Messiah.

He felt that, if he wanted to be a wandering missionary, he would have to know various languages. He already knew Latin, Persian, and Aramaic, but he entered the University of Vienna to study Arabic as well as church history and theology. From there he went to another university to continue his studies in Oriental languages. Because of his earlier contact with Roman Catholic friends, he went to Rome to study in the college. But he could not accept some of the things that he was taught there, and he soon left. In leaving, he was branded as one who was dangerous in his theology. As a result of this encounter he decided that his Bible was to be his sole guide for doctrine and living. He wandered throughout Europe and finally offered his services to the London Society. He again studied theology; but, after two years, studies proved to be too much for him; he was too much of a wanderer.

He left England in 1821 and visited a number of eastern Mediterranean cities. In rapid succession, he was in Alexandria, Cairo, Jaffa, Acre, Beruit, and finally Jerusalem. In Cairo he visited the Karaites, since he had a special affinity toward them. As we have seen already, they were the group who accepted only the Scriptures of the Old Testament.

This appealed to Wolff, and he distributed a number of New Testaments among them. In 1882 he found himself in Jerusalem reasoning with Jewish people in the synagogues. He remained there several months, distributing copies of the Hebrew New Testament. From there he went back to Egypt and then returned again to Jerusalem, preaching the Word to Jewish people from morning until night. His health gave way under the strain, and he had to rest for a while. Soon after, however, he was off on his journeys again, to Damascus and from there to Baghdad. Surprisingly, many rabbis did not resent Wolff's efforts and gladly took New Testaments. In other areas he suffered greatly, and in his travels he was much like the apostle Paul, "in perils often."

He was back again in Jerusalem in 1829, and with great difficulty he managed to open a school and to preach to both Jewish people and the Greeks. This did not last long because of the opposition that began to grow against him. His restless nature drove him to further travels across the Middle East. In due time he reached India, and in his efforts to preach the word there he was stripped of everything he had. He was undaunted, however, and continued again to cover the Middle East in his preaching activities. A great number of Jewish people did accept Jesus as the Messiah and Saviour.

Eventually, because of ill health, he returned to the British Isles, where he was ordained in Dublin in 1838. His friend Henry Drummond said to him, "You are as fit for a parish priest as I am for a dancing master." There is also the story that, as he was to take his first pastorate, the resigning minister of the church preached a sermon on the text, "After me ravening wolves will come and devour the flock"! In spite of all the prophecies of his failure, he proved to be a faithful pastor beloved by his members. He died in 1862 after an amazing ministry as apostle to Jewish people across the Middle East and faithful service as pastor in the British Isles.

THE PRESENT-DAY SITUATION

The past few years have seen a number of indications that the Lord is speaking to many Jewish hearts. The Jesus Movement has drawn many Jewish young people. Some have estimated that Jewish believers make up 25 percent of this movement. A number of magazines have given coverage to the phenomenon of a growing member of Jewish people who believe in Jesus the Messiah. William Willoughby, religious news editor of the *Washington Evening Star,* wrote an article, "A Breakthrough for Messianic Judaism," which was featured in the March 1972 issue of *Moody Monthly.* He indicated that we must be cautious and not allow enthusiasm to distort the picture of Jewish people coming to the Messiah; but he did state, "If the rate of speed for new believers continues for the next ten years as it has for the past decade, then there will be little doubt that it will be considered a significant movement toward Christ." He cites Edward Plowman, author of *The Jesus Movement in America,* who indicated that Messianic Judaism could very well become "another major Jewish denomination, along with the Conservative, Orthodox, Reform, and the growing Reconstructionist schools."[7]

As mentioned in chapter 11, there are groups of Jewish believers in the land of Israel. These developments are causing the Jewish people to ask serious questions. It is necessary that the Church be apprised of the situation and be ready and willing to share its faith. Each opportunity is significant as we sense that the age is drawing to a close. Without hesitation we can say we are grateful to God for the events of this day, realizing that, as national Israel begins to stir under God's working, their acceptance is "life from the dead" (Ro 11:15).

7. William Willoughby, "A Breakthrough for Messianic Judaism," *Moody Monthly,* March 1972, p. 29.

FOR FURTHER STUDY

Bernstein, A. *Some Jewish Witnesses for Christ.* London: Operative Jewish Converts' Inst., 1909.

Dunlop, John. *Memories of Gospel Triumphs Among the Jews During the Victorian Era.* London: Partridge, 1894.

Einspruch, Henry, ed. *Would I, Would You?* Baltimore, Md.: Lewish & Harriet Lederer Fdn., 1970.

Stevens, George H. *Jewish Christian Leaders.* London: Oliphants, 1966.

Willoughby, William. "A Breakthrough for Messianic Judaism?" *Moody Monthly,* March 1972.

11

RELIGIOUS ATTITUDES IN MODERN ISRAEL

The establishment of the state of Israel and its continued existence, though unfortunately surrounded by unfriendly neighbors, is striking evidence that history is moving in the very direction indicated by biblical prophecy.

In 1973, after twenty-five years of statehood, Israel had a population of over three million. Seemingly impossible strides have been made in reclaiming and settling the land, building industry, and creating a distinctly Jewish life and culture. The old city of Jerusalem is again under Jewish control.

But are there other, less apparent evidences of movement toward end-time conditions?

THE BIBLE

One of the most significant evidences, in my judgment, is the Israelis' keen interest in the Bible. Classroom Bible study is provided in state schools. Younger children study the lives of the patriarchs and other famous Bible men. Junior high school instruction centers on biblical history and geography, often with entire classes visiting the actual biblical sites. For those able to attend high school after the tenth grade (the last two years are on a tuition basis), Bible instruction centers on prophecy and morals. Many students in the university take courses in the New Testament.

This interest includes the New Testament and may well

be a first step in what God will one day bring to pass. Consider, for example, the fact that the Bible is taught in Israel's schools. The synoptic gospels (Matthew, Mark, and Luke) are studied on the Junior high school level for a life of Jesus. While many traditional Jews have opposed this project, these studies have met with enthusiastic response by most Israelis. The plan is to expand the program.

Such exposure is important. As students and their teachers read the Word of God, the Spirit of God has opportunity to speak through its promises. Some will see their spiritual need and find Him. Certainly a large segment of the younger generations will acquire Bible knowledge that will be a basis for understanding the future unfolding of prophecy. This is in contrast to many American Jewish people, who know very little about the Bible.

Israel's leaders see the Bible as important in helping their people discover their heritage as well as their future. One tangible evidence of this interest is the projected construction of a building in Jerusalem to be known as *Beit Hatenach* (House of the Bible). The government of Israel and the Jewish National Fund have already allocated an area in the southern part of the city for this structure. It will serve as a center for the discussion and study of biblical materials for Jews, Christians, and Muslims.

The building will include an artifacts pavilion, a section for Bible texts in printed and manuscript form, and a library large enough to store a million volumes of biblical materials and commentaries. David Ben Gurion was keenly interested in this project, and there is already on the part of some an anticipation of the fulfillment of an earlier prophet's vision that "out of Zion shall go forth the law, and the word of the LORD from Jerusalem" (Isaiah 2:3, KJV).

SECULAR SIGNS

There are other signs of quickening interest in religion.

Most of the population are secular and can be termed agnostic. Although they are not atheistic, they are not religiously oriented and are reluctant to accept the authority of the Talmud. Thousands of Israelis flout its religious authority in such ways as flocking to the beach on the Sabbath. Secularists also emphasize the role of man rather than the role of God in explaining the rise of their nation.

Even among this group, however, there is a restlessness indicating an attempt to reevaluate their position in the light of the culture of a Bible and a Talmud. What seems to be a heightened sensitivity of the secular conscience is possibly due to the reading and study of the Old Testament in the schools.

Many of the secularists as well as the more liberal among the religious take an interest in the gospels and in Jesus. In various degrees Jesus is respected, admired, and regarded as a great prophet. One prominent person indicated to me that many in Israel are reading books and studying His life. He noted that such an attitude and interest had not been possible until recent years.

Some of the very religious, apprehensive about creeping modernization and growing laxity in Sabbath observance, have organized demonstrations and even stoned buses and cars operating before the Sabbath is officially over. Such reactions, however, are the expression of a small minority.

The Six Day War in 1967 saw some quickening of interest in spiritual things among the secular group. This interest was heightened even further in the Yom Kippur War of 1973. It is to be hoped that through the bitter experiences of war, along with the biblical instruction in the schools, the secular Jewish people will turn more and more to Scripture and trust its promises.

A process of preparation and education seems to be under way. As a result, many are becoming familiar with the facts of the gospels and are thinking through the Bible's great claims and assertions; and, it is to be hoped, they will come to significant conclusions.

THE RELIGIOUS

Many among the religious feel that the redemption of Israel has already begun. The Wailing Wall—or Western Wall, as it is now called—is a center for all kinds of religious observances as well as daybreak classes in Bible and Talmud. Bar-Ilan University, the country's religiously oriented institution of higher learning, makes an important contribution by combining traditional religious values with contemporary education.

Interest in religion is latent but easily aroused. On the bus, in the park, in restaurants, and in other public places, the conversation can quickly swing to religious and biblical subjects. One person may hold that the Messiah is not a person; another may insist that He is. Someone will say that the Messianic age has arrived; others will stress that hard days are ahead in the period of "the foot of the Messiah"— that is, in the period just before He is to appear.

THE MESSIANIC JEW

In addition to the influence of both religious and secular elements of the population, Israel today is being affected by Messianic Jews, those who accept the claims of Jesus as Messiah. An Israeli dictionary defines them as "a sect of Jews who have declared themselves as Jews in their nationality and for their faithfulness to the State of Israel and as Christians in their religious expression."

The status of the Messianic Jew poses problems. The traditional Jew is unlikely to accept the Messianic Jew as Jewish. However, the Messianic Jew is dissatisfied with the government's definition of a Christian: a non-Jew. No Messianic Jew wants to be known as a non-Jew. (Although it is the Orthodox Jew who causes the government to make the definition of the Messianic Jew as a non-Jew.) Furthermore, the government lumps the various denominations into the general category of "Christian"; and here again the Messianic Jew does not want to be lumped with this group and lose his distinctiveness and his tie with his people. The government recognizes only the Orthodox or traditional Jewish people, thereby denying legal status to marriages, funerals, and estates of the Conservative, Reform, or Messianic Jews, although those belonging to these groups may be citizens and have religious freedom to worship as they please. It is no wonder that the question Who is a Jew? has not been answered to the satisfaction of everyone.

Though reluctant to adopt Western modes of Christianity, Messianic Jews hold weekly worship services much like those of the New Testament believers. They meet during the week for Bible study and prayer, and also hold youth conferences. A national fellowship of Messianic Jews seeks to communicate their faith in a context which Jewish people will understand.

Messianic Jews have a twofold purpose. First, they wish to share their beliefs so that their fellow Jews will respond to the claims of Jesus. Second, they are endeavoring to sow the seed of the Word of God as part of the preparation of their nation for the day when the Messiah will come and Israel will have its prophetically promised place among the nations.

These, then, are a few of the currents in Israel today which suggest that God is preparing His people for the events described in prophecy. It is easy to believe that the world may be nearing the times prophesied by kings, priests, and statesmen when Israel will be readied to meet the Ancient of Days. Certainly the words of the inspired men are once more being heard and considered in the land of the regathered people.

FOR FURTHER STUDY

BOOKS

Arberry, A. J., ed. *Religions in the Middle East.* 3 vols. Cambridge: U. Press, 1969. This set includes volume I, *Judaism and Christianity;* volume II, *Islam;* and volume III, *The Three Religions in Concord and Conflict.*

Bamberger, B. J. *The Bible, a Modern Jewish Approach.* New York: Schocken, 1963.

Louvish, Misha, ed. *Facts About Israel, 1973.* Jerusalem: Keter, 1973. This is published yearly and can be obtained from any Israel Government Tourist Office. There is one chapter that treats the people of Israel in the religious communities and religious holidays.

Sachar, Howard. *From the Ends of the Earth, the People of Israel.* New York: Dell, 1970.

Samuel, Edwin. *Structure of Society in Israel.* New York: Random, 1969.

Weiner, H. *The Wild Goats of Ein Gedi: Religious and Philosophical Trends.* Garden City, N.Y.: Doubleday, 1961.

FILMSTRIPS

Religion and Culture in Israel. The Land of Israel series, no. 10. New Rochelle, N.Y.: Pathescope Ed. Films.

FILMS

Israel—Twentieth-Century Miracle. Chicago: Amer. Assoc. for Jewish Evang.